Vagrant: Up and Running

Mitchell Hashimoto

Beijing · Cambridge · Farnham · Köln · Sebastopol · Tokyo

Vagrant: Up and Running

by Mitchell Hashimoto

Printed in the United States of America.

Published by O'Reilly Media, Inc., 1005 Gravenstein Highway North, Sebastopol, CA 95472.

O'Reilly books may be purchased for educational, business, or sales promotional use. Online editions are also available for most titles (*http://my.safaribooksonline.com*). For more information, contact our corporate/institutional sales department: 800-998-9938 or *corporate@oreilly.com*.

Editors: Mike Loukides and Courtney Nash
Production Editor: Kristen Borg
Proofreader: Jasmine Kwityn
Indexer: Fred Brown
Cover Designer: Randy Comer
Interior Designer: David Futato
Illustrator: Rebecca Demarest

June 2013:   First Edition

Revision History for the First Edition:

2013-05-28:   First release

See *http://oreilly.com/catalog/errata.csp?isbn=9781449335830* for release details.

ISBN: 978-1-449-33583-0

[LSI]

Table of Contents

Foreword

Every so often, you encounter software that immediately strikes you with its combination of clarity, simplicity, power, and usefulness. You simultaneously say "wow!" and "why didn't I think of that?" But you couldn't have thought of it. It needs an author who can conceive and implement that particular vision, not just appreciate it. Vagrant is that kind of software, and Mitchell Hashimoto is that kind of author.

Software as a service dramatically lowers the cost of change for its users. As a result, they come to expect near-instantaneous responsiveness from software vendors. The ability to continuously deliver new features is taking its place alongside the features themselves as a competitive advantage. Service providers face the conundrum of needing to accelerate velocity without sacrificing quality. Vagrant provides a critical contribution to solving that problem.

Agility experts often talk about John Boyd's OODA (Observe-Orient-Decide-Act) Loop. An Air Force pilot, Boyd developed the OODA Loop concept to describe the process of reacting to an enemy during airborne battle. Victory came from "getting inside your enemy's OODA Loop"—in other words, being able to react, respond, and change more quickly than your enemy.

Approaching software delivery as a form of battle requiring fast reflexes conjures up visions of fear, tension, and sweat. But fear and tension lead to mistakes (aka bugs). How do you get inside your competition's OODA Loop without working 24 hours a day or permanently raising your blood pressure? The answer lies in automation.

Automation lets you wring unnecessary manual effort, along with opportunities for mistakes, out of the process. It also allows you to move faster without worrying about getting things wrong or leaving things out. Consistent automation throughout the software lifecycle further reduces chances of mistakes due to variation. If you test your software against exactly the same system configuration that's running in production, you're more likely to catch the right bugs, and less likely to waste time fixing the wrong ones.

Vagrant brings configuration automation all the way down to the developer's desktop. With it, you can package the same operating system that runs in production—along with the same configuration automation scripts—in a form that's easily shared among developers. Instead of spending the first two days on the job installing software, a new development team member can spin up a production-identical environment on their laptop simply by typing vagrant init then vagrant up.

With Vagrant, a new developer can get started delivering value in an hour instead of a day. All the developers on the team can update their environments with a new software version in minutes, instead of hours, simply by typing vagrant provision. Then they can all get back to valuable work, secure in the knowledge they're all building against the same version as production and as each other. In other words, they can go faster, without fear.

I like to think of Vagrant as the Git of development clouds. Centralized development and test environments create bottlenecks. Vagrant lets developers work at their own pace and in their own environment, while keeping all the environments synchronized with each other. Flexibility joined with consistency is the best and sanest way to tighten a team's OODA Loop.

Finally, in addition to writing great software, Mitchell has always done a good job of writing documentation. The Getting Started tutorial on the Vagrant website is a great way to…well, get started. This book continues the tradition of helpful Vagrant documentation. It's useful for beginners and experts alike. It does a great job of balancing basic concepts with behind-the-scenes technical details. Even experienced Vagrant users will learn some new tricks. Just as Vagrant belongs in your Continuous Delivery toolkit, so too *Vagrant: Up and Running* belongs on your bookshelf.

—Jeff Sussna
Founder and Principal, Ingineering.IT
DevOps/Continuous Delivery Coaching and Implementation
http://www.ingineering.it

Preface

Vagrant is quickly becoming a must-have tool in every software and operation engineer's toolbox. Used by tens of thousands of companies, the Vagrant workflow is a familiar and highly praised way to build, manage, and distribute automatically created development and test environments. These environments are identical whether you're working on Mac OS X, Windows, or Linux.

Vagrant takes the cloud, a revolutionary movement founded on the idea of cheap, disposable computing resources, and makes this idea available on anyone's desktop. With just two commands and zero configuration, Vagrant automatically builds and configures a fully featured virtual machine for any purpose.

And with just a little bit of easy-to-learn configuration, Vagrant can automatically set up complex network configurations, install and manage software within the virtual machine, or package the virtual machine for re-use by other people.

Virtualization is the foundational technology behind what is often referred to as the cloud. Amazon Web Services (*http://aws.amazon.com/*), Microsoft Azure (*http://www.windowsazure.com/*), virtual private server (VPS) providers (*http://en.wikipedia.org/wiki/Virtual_private_server*), and more are based completely around this technology or those similar to it. These sort of cloud services are now the de facto standard for hosting web applications.

Virtualization is everywhere. The good news is that virtualization technology is readily available to anyone with a modern computer. The bad news is that we're only at the tip of the iceberg of what is possible with this technology. Vagrant is here to change this.

In early 2010, I worked for a web development consultancy and was frustrated by having to repeatedly set up development environments manually for various projects. I approached John Bender, who was facing similar frustrations at the time, and the project was started.

The first version of Vagrant was released in March 2010. From the beginning, Vagrant was open sourced under the MIT license. In October 2010, Engine Yard announced that they were going to sponsor the Vagrant project. With the support from Engine Yard, I was able to travel around the country to various conferences and speak about Vagrant.

Slowly, more and more people started to use and talk about Vagrant. These early adopters of Vagrant were active in reporting bugs, requesting features, and pointing out any improvements that could be made. Hundreds of early users contributed code and documentation back to the project.

Vagrant 1.0, the first stable version, was released in March 2012, exactly two years after the original version of Vagrant. Despite not releasing an official stable release prior, hundreds of companies were already using Vagrant at that point and had proven 1.0 to be stable.

Today, Vagrant is used by companies worldwide who have found great benefits in integrating Vagrant into their developer or operations workflows. It is difficult to attend any cloud or IT infrastructure conference without hearing Vagrant mentioned or discussed. And yet, Vagrant is still very young. I have full confidence that in just a few more years, Vagrant will become a necessary tool for any developer or operations engineer.

Conventions Used in This Book

The following typographical conventions are used in this book:

Italic
> Indicates new terms, URLs, email addresses, filenames, and file extensions.

`Constant width`
> Used for program listings, as well as within paragraphs to refer to program elements such as variable or function names, databases, data types, environment variables, statements, and keywords.

`Constant width bold`
> Shows commands or other text that should be typed literally by the user.

`Constant width italic`
> Shows text that should be replaced with user-supplied values or by values determined by context.

 This icon signifies a tip, suggestion, or general note.

 This icon indicates a warning or caution.

Using Code Examples

This book is here to help you get your job done. In general, if this book includes code examples, you may use the code in this book in your programs and documentation. You do not need to contact us for permission unless you're reproducing a significant portion of the code. For example, writing a program that uses several chunks of code from this book does not require permission. Selling or distributing a CD-ROM of examples from O'Reilly books does require permission. Answering a question by citing this book and quoting example code does not require permission. Incorporating a significant amount of example code from this book into your product's documentation does require permission.

We appreciate, but do not require, attribution. An attribution usually includes the title, author, publisher, and ISBN. For example: "*Vagrant: Up and Running* by Mitchell Hashimoto (O'Reilly). Copyright 2013 Mitchell Hashimoto, 978-1-449-33583-0."

If you feel your use of code examples falls outside fair use or the permission given above, feel free to contact us at *permissions@oreilly.com*.

Safari® Books Online

 Safari Books Online is an on-demand digital library that delivers expert content in both book and video form from the world's leading authors in technology and business.

Technology professionals, software developers, web designers, and business and creative professionals use Safari Books Online as their primary resource for research, problem solving, learning, and certification training.

Safari Books Online offers a range of product mixes and pricing programs for organizations, government agencies, and individuals. Subscribers have access to thousands of books, training videos, and prepublication manuscripts in one fully searchable database from publishers like O'Reilly Media, Prentice Hall Professional, Addison-Wesley Professional, Microsoft Press, Sams, Que, Peachpit Press, Focal Press, Cisco Press, John Wiley & Sons, Syngress, Morgan Kaufmann, IBM Redbooks, Packt, Adobe Press, FT Press, Apress, Manning, New Riders, McGraw-Hill, Jones & Bartlett, Course Technology, and dozens more. For more information about Safari Books Online, please visit us online.

How to Contact Us

Please address comments and questions concerning this book to the publisher:

O'Reilly Media, Inc.
1005 Gravenstein Highway North
Sebastopol, CA 95472
800-998-9938 (in the United States or Canada)
707-829-0515 (international or local)
707-829-0104 (fax)

We have a web page for this book, where we list errata, examples, and any additional information. You can access this page at *http://oreil.ly/vagrant_up_running*.

To comment or ask technical questions about this book, send email to *bookques tions@oreilly.com*.

For more information about our books, courses, conferences, and news, see our website at *http://www.oreilly.com*.

Find us on Facebook: *http://facebook.com/oreilly*

Follow us on Twitter: *http://twitter.com/oreillymedia*

Watch us on YouTube: *http://www.youtube.com/oreillymedia*

Acknowledgements

Although my name is on the cover, the existence of this book is thanks to many people, both directly and indirectly. Writing this book came at a particularly busy time in my life, full of both professional and personal changes, and I have many people to thank.

I want to first thank the Vagrant community, which continues to motivate and inspire me daily to build the best tools I can. The community is friendly and knowledgeable—and teaches me new things about my own tool almost daily.

Specifically, I want to thank John Bender. John has believed in this project since I first told him the idea over instant messenger, and his passion for the project has only grown since then. Thanks for believing and always pushing me to make Vagrant the best it can be.

I would like to thank a few individuals for reviewing early copies of this book and contributing many helpful suggestions and improvements to my work: Robby Colvin, Matt Stine, and Jeff Sussna. Each of these individuals has been a dedicated Vagrant user for a long time, and their careful eye and experience as Vagrant educators helped shape this book into a truly great learning resource.

Thanks to my editor, Courtney Nash, and the fantastic staff at O'Reilly for their help in the preparation of this book. Courtney's never-ending presence at every conference I attended was a constant reminder I had a book to write (and more importantly, finish).

Without guidance from my parents, I would never have had the discipline or drive to achieve what I have, including this book. For everything they've taught me and showed me along the way, thank you.

Finally, I wrote this book just as I was starting a new company, speaking at dozens of conferences, shipping the biggest Vagrant release ever, and more. For patience while I pushed through these large tasks, continuously showing me the value of maintaining good balance between work and family, and being one of my biggest supporters, I want to thank Amy, who I love very much. Through good and bad, you're always there making everything just… better. Thank you so much. It's time to take a vacation and spend some quality relaxation time in Hawaii!

CHAPTER 1

An Introduction to Vagrant

Vagrant is a tool for building complete development environments, sandboxed in a virtual machine. Vagrant lowers development environment setup time, increases development/production parity, and brings the idea of disposable compute resources down to the desktop.

With one command, Vagrant does all of the following:

- Creates a virtual machine for you based on an operating system of your choice.
- Modifies the physical properties of this virtual machine (e.g., RAM, number of CPUs, etc.).
- Establishes network interfaces so that you can access your virtual machine from your own computer, another device on the same network, or even from another virtual machine.
- Sets up shared folders so that you can continue editing files on your own machine and have those modifications mirror over to the guest machine.
- Boots the virtual machine so that it is running.
- Sets the hostname of the machine, since a lot of software depends on this being properly set.
- Provisions software on the machine via a shell script or configuration management solution such as Chef (*http://www.opscode.com/chef/*), Puppet (*http://puppet labs.com/puppet/what-is-puppet/*), or a custom solution.
- Performs host and guest specific tweaking to work around known issues that may arise. For example, Ubuntu 12.04 LTS breaks VirtualBox networking defaults, so Vagrant makes minor modifications to some configuration in Ubuntu to make sure networking continues working. Vagrant does these sorts of things for many host/ guest pairs.

This is all completed in about a minute, but the time it takes can greatly increase depending on the software being installed.

Once Vagrant finishes setting up the machine, you are left with a completely sandboxed, fully provisioned development environment. Due to the shared folders and networking, you continue using your own editor and your own browser to develop and test your applications, but the code itself runs on the virtual machine.

Vagrant handles the entire lifecycle of the machine for you, so in addition to setting up your development environment, Vagrant can do all of the following:

- SSH into the machine.
- Halt (shut down) the machine.
- Destroy the machine, completely deleting its virtual hard drive and metadata.
- Suspend or resume the machine.
- Package the machine state so that you can distribute it to other developers.

Vagrant is a Swiss Army knife for development environments. It does everything you need to create and manage them, and helps enforce good practices by encouraging the use of automation and an environment that more closely resembles production.

If there is something Vagrant can't do with your development environments, chances are that you can extend Vagrant's behavior through a plug-in to achieve what you need. If this ends up being something that a lot of people need, then your plug-in could be merged back into Vagrant core, since Vagrant itself is open source. Thus, by using Vagrant, you're using a tool that thousands of developers have contributed to based on their real-world needs.

Why Vagrant?

In order to understand the need for a tool like Vagrant, it is important to understand the old ways that Vagrant is trying to replace. Prior to Vagrant, the preferred method of working on a web application was to install and configure all the software you needed (e.g., Apache, MySQL, RabbitMQ, etc.) locally on your development machine.

I admit that in the days when web applications were almost certainly just PHP and MySQL alone, this made a lot of sense. Once installed, both technologies are generally "set and forget" and they just work. They also work well with multiple projects due to easy virtual hosts in Apache and database isolation with MySQL.

But today, modern web applications have a lot more moving parts, a lot more options for underlying technologies, and a lot more overall complexity. While PHP and MySQL are still very popular, they no longer clearly dominate the market, and languages like JavaScript, Python, and Ruby are quickly becoming the dynamic languages of choice.

For databases, there are now a handful of choices that are equally correct in their valid use case (e.g., MySQL, PostgreSQL, Redis, Riak, Cassandra, etc.). In addition to just languages and databases, there are multiple web servers, application servers, and back-end services each with their own use cases (e.g., Apache, Nginx, Unicorn, Thin, RabbitMQ, Solr, etc.).

The various combinations of these technologies that may be used quickly becomes out of hand, and keeping everything properly configured and installed locally is a nightmare. There are other issues with the local install practice as well:

- Everything must be installed manually, by a human. Installing some of the aforementioned software is not at all trivial, especially on Mac OS X and Windows, the primary development platforms. A lot of the software doesn't even compile or run on Windows at all!

- Configuration is even more difficult than installation. Once the software is installed, it has to be configured. Developers are unlikely to know how to configure it to best resemble production. Misconfigured software can lead to functionality that appears to work in development, but doesn't work the same in production.

- With manually set up development environments, there is a stark difference between development and production. This leads to a lot of "works on my machine" bugs (i.e., bugs that don't appear on a developer's machine, but appear in production). Ideally, development would mirror production identically.

- Multiple projects are difficult to impossible, because each project usually requires slightly different configurations of their services, or can require completely different backend systems. The result is either a brittle setup of poorly configured dependencies, or a system that is running a lot of services that each individual web application may not need. It all gets messy very quickly.

- It's difficult to keep development environments in sync with other team members, or to bring a new team member on board. Because each developer is responsible for a separate development environment, it is easy for the environments to quickly get out of sync. And when new team members are hired, they are personally responsible for manually setting up an entire complex development environment. The result is confusion and long onboarding times before new team members can actually start working on the project itself.

- It's difficult for multiple developers to use different operating systems. Some server software is very difficult or impossible to run on certain operating systems. Therefore, developers are stuck mostly using the operating system that is best documented for setting up their development environment.

Vagrant is a modern solution to all of these problems. While not strictly required, Vagrant encourages automation to set up your development environments using shell scripts or configuration management software. Vagrant allows you to work with the same operating system that is running in production, whether your physical development machine is running Linux, Mac OS X, or Windows. Because Vagrant puts your development environment into a virtual machine, working with multiple projects is easy, because each project just get its own virtual machine. Finally, working with a team is easier than ever, since you can share the virtual machine image. And bringing a new team member on board is as simple as telling them to build their Vagrant machine with a single command.

The Tao of Vagrant

Before even installing Vagrant or seeing how it works, it is important to understand the high-level workflow of Vagrant in an actual working environment. These principles are collectively known as "the Tao of Vagrant."

In a world with Vagrant, developers can check out any repository from version control, run `vagrant up`, and have a fully running development environment without any human interaction. Developers continue to work on their own machines, in the comfort of their own editors, browsers, and other tools. The existence of Vagrant is transparent and unimportant in the mind of the developer. Vagrant is the workhorse that creates consistent and stable development environments.

System operations engineers work on system automation scripts, again using their choice of editors and tools on their own machines. When they're ready to test these scripts, they `vagrant up`, and have a complete sandbox matching production, ready to test real-world scenarios and system automation.

The automation developed by system operations engineers is not only used in production, but also in development. With every `vagrant up`, developers are getting fully provisioned development environments using the same scripts that are used to set up production. This way, developers work in environments that mimic production as closely as possible.

If something goes wrong, or they just want to start over from a clean slate, developers and operations engineers can run `vagrant destroy`, which removes all traces of that development environment from their machines. Then a `vagrant up` again will re-create an identical, fully functioning development environment in a snap.

At the end of the day, Vagrant can suspend, halt, or destroy the development environment, keeping the overall system clean. Never again can developers forget to shut down a stray server process and waste precious compute resources. When ready, `vagrant up` will bring back a ready-to-go development environment in just a few minutes.

The best part of all this is that this knowledge transfers to *every* project. Whether working on project A, project B, or even at company A or company B, as long as they follow the

Tao of Vagrant, the workflow is exactly the same. As a result, productivity abounds and "works on my machine" bugs disappear.

Of course, it isn't necessary to follow each and every principle of the Tao of Vagrant to use Vagrant. Vagrant is a general-purpose tool and can be molded into your environment as you see fit. But it is important to see and understand the larger vision behind Vagrant.

Alternatives to Vagrant

There are various ways to achieve what Vagrant does using other technologies. Each of the following alternatives provide some of Vagrant's functionality, but no solution can match Vagrant feature for feature. And perhaps the biggest disadvantage of all is losing the workflow Vagrant enforces, forcing you to invent your own or mimic the workflow of Vagrant as closely as possible.

Prior to Vagrant 1.1, the top reason people looked for alternatives was because Vagrant was tied to VirtualBox (*https://www.virtualbox.org/*). However, since version 1.1, Vagrant can work with any virtualization layer, with official support for options such as VMware. Vagrant can even work with remote environments such as Amazon's Elastic Compute Cloud (EC2).

Plain Desktop Virtualization

Vagrant is a layer on top of some virtualization solution. Instead, you could use that virtualization solution directly. VirtualBox is free, but there are also many commercial alternatives (e.g., VMware, Parallels, etc.). Each of these can be used to mimic what Vagrant does.

It is standard practice for this software to support sharing or exporting virtual machines, shared folders, port forwarding, and so on. It is completely possible to do everything Vagrant does with these tools. The major downside is that the approach to do this would be completely manual, and cross-platform support would be nontrivial. Additionally, you lose the predictable Vagrant workflow.

If you have a very specific goal and are OK with losing the benefits Vagrant offers, then this is a reasonable solution.

Containers

Another approach is to use container-based solutions such as LXC or OpenVZ.

Containers don't provide full virtualization but instead are super-powered isolated environments running the same kernel. A big benefit of containers is that they don't incur the same overhead as virtualization, since they run just like any other process on your machine. A downside of containers is that you can only run the same kernel that is running on your host system, so you can't have a Windows container on Linux, for example.

For some work environments, this is not an issue, but there is another major negative aspect of containers for development. Containers are highly specific to the host operating system. Linux supports LXC and OpenVZ, while FreeBSD supports Jails. OS X provides no container support, and neither does Windows. Therefore, container usage requires an entire team to use the same host operating system.

In general, containers are ideal for production usage, since they offer a reasonably secure way to isolate resources within the same operating system without performance overhead. But for development, containers impose strict limitations that are often hard to work with.

Cloud

Another approach is to ditch desktop virtualization altogether and do development directly in the cloud, such as on EC2.

The main benefit of this approach is that it allows developers to work from incredibly low-powered desktop machines in an environment that closely resembles production. It is also possible to mimic much more advanced production environments, since the remote machines can be much more powerful than a typical development machine.

The disadvantage here is that this approach requires an Internet connection, and it can have a much higher financial cost associated with it.

If your organization is at the point where they have enough automation to support this sort of remote work, it is generally quite easy to make the switch to Vagrant, if possible.

Setting Up Vagrant

After learning about Vagrant, what it can do, the benefits it has to offer, and a small history behind it, it's time to actually install it so we can get up and running with our first virtual machine!

This chapter covers what is required to install Vagrant on Linux, Mac OS X, and Windows operating systems. Vagrant must be installed on every computer that you want to run Vagrant-created development environments. If you're working in a team environment, laptops are usually distributed with Vagrant preinstalled (or, if not, it should be one of the first software components to be installed).

Vagrant behaves identically across Linux, Mac OS X, and Windows, so your developers can work on the operating system they feel most productive on. No more nightmares setting up Linux services on Windows!

If you're using Vagrant with VirtualBox, then VirtualBox must be installed separately. If you forget this step, Vagrant will give you a nice error message telling you to install it. VirtualBox is the only thing other than Vagrant that must be installed for Vagrant to function properly.

The order in which you install these components doesn't matter, since if you install Vagrant first Vagrant will just give you an error message about missing VirtualBox. If you install VirtualBox first, you won't have Vagrant yet. Either way, the setup process is order independent.

Installing VirtualBox

To get started, I recommend installing VirtualBox first. VirtualBox is open source and cross-platform virtualization software from Oracle. It is available for Linux, Mac OS X, Windows, and other platforms that Vagrant doesn't explicitly support.

VirtualBox can be downloaded from *http://virtualbox.org*. VirtualBox provides installers and packages for Windows, Mac OS X, and various distributions of Linux. If you can't find a package for your operating system, then you can compile VirtualBox from source.

At the time of writing, Vagrant supports VirtualBox versions 4.0.x, 4.1.x, and 4.2.x. The Vagrant 1.0 release will support up to but not including VirtualBox 5.0. Note that you should always use the latest version of Vagrant in order to get the best compatibility with VirtualBox.

Installing VirtualBox also requires setting up a kernel driver for your operating system. The kernel driver is responsible for some low-level virtualization help, makes shared folders possible, optimizes network operating with VirtualBox, and more.

On Windows and Mac OS X, the installation of the driver happens automatically.

On Linux, you may need to install extra packages and run an extra command in order to set it up. Extra packages generally include kernel headers, DKMS (Dynamic Kernel Module System), and perhaps others. The VirtualBox installation process should tell you if you're missing anything. To set up the kernel drivers on Linux, run `/etc/init.d/ vboxdrv setup` as root.

On all platforms, it is highly recommended that you restart your computer after installing VirtualBox, just to make sure the kernel driver starts up cleanly. This is especially important if you're installing VirtualBox over a previous version, since VirtualBox has been known to be finicky with replacing prior kernel drivers without a restart.

Installing Vagrant

Like VirtualBox, Vagrant is distributed as a set of packages and installers for various platforms. For this book, we'll be working with the latest 1.x series. This release series builds on top of the 1.0.x stable series and is essentially a beta series toward a stable version 2.0.

Despite technically being a beta series, most companies quickly adopt the latest version of Vagrant because Vagrant has a history of being quite stable and each release introduces impressive improvements and better support for every combination of host and guest operating system.

The installers for every platform can be found at *http://downloads.vagrantup.com*. Open this in your browser and make sure you're on the page listing the downloads for the latest version matching 1.x (where *x* of course is not a literal x, but some number).

Prior to the installation packages, Vagrant was distributed as a RubyGem. Installation packages are now the preferred way to install Vagrant, so you should uninstall the RubyGem version and follow the instructions for your platform. The RubyGem-based installation is still supported for Vagrant 1.0.x, but is deprecated and will not be supported in any future versions.

Next, we'll cover the specifics of installing Vagrant on each supported platform.

Vagrant Versions and Release Cycle

By understanding how Vagrant versioning works, you can know when it is safe to upgrade, when backward compatibility issues may be introduced, and so on. Vagrant follows a predictable versioning pattern and release cycle.

Vagrant versions are in the format of X.Y.Z where X is the major version number, Y is the minor version number, and Z is the patch number. A change in any of these numbers has different meanings.

Most importantly, any version in the format of X.0.Z (where the minor version number is a zero) represents a stable release. These releases can be trusted to have been used in production for long periods of time and proven stable and battle hardened. Therefore, versions such as 1.0.0 or 1.0.5 are stable versions. Differences in the other numbers will be covered shortly.

The major number represents major changes, often ones that are backward-incompatible to prior major versions. Therefore, between a version 1.0.0 and 2.0.0, one can expect major changes in both the usage and configuration of Vagrant. Note, however, that there is an exception with Vagrant. Vagrant promises to maintain backward compatibility with the Vagrantfile format of every major version.

This means that your Vagrantfile for Vagrant 1.0 should work with Vagrant 2.0, or Vagrant should at least give helpful messages identifying features that may not exist anymore. Things won't just crash.

Next, any change in the minor number represents a new release toward the next major number version. For example, version 1.2.0 would be a release working toward 2.0.0. These versions are typically less stable (though not unstable), contain new experimental features, and may have backward incompatibilities. These releases should be used if you're interested in the latest features with relative stability, but you may experience bugs here and there.

Finally, any change in the patch number is just a minor bug fix and is always safe to upgrade to. Backward incompatibilities are never introduced and only new features that pose absolutely zero risk to existing stability may be introduced. Features are never removed.

If you're ever unsure which version to use, go with the latest stable release. If you're interested in upgrading, reading the changelog is recommended. The changelog can be found in the Vagrant source repository on GitHub.

Mac OS X

Installation of Vagrant on OS X follows a standard process, so if OS X is your primary machine, this should be very comfortable for you.

Find the Mac OS X installer from the downloads page opened previously, and download it to the computer on which you'd like to install Vagrant. Just as you've likely done time and time again, double-click the DMG to mount it, double-click the installer in the mounted folder, and follow the installation steps. The installer should look like Figure 1-1, a familiar Mac OS X package. The whole process should take no more than a few minutes.

Vagrant installs itself to */Applications/Vagrant*, right alongside the other applications installed on your computer. Vagrant also puts a *vagrant* executable into */usr/bin* so it is available by default from the terminal.

To verify everything worked correctly, open up a terminal and type `vagrant --version`. You should see output containing the Vagrant version you just downloaded. Just so you're sure, you should see something similar to Figure 1-2, although the version number may be slightly different depending on what the latest version is. If everything looks right, you're ready to go!

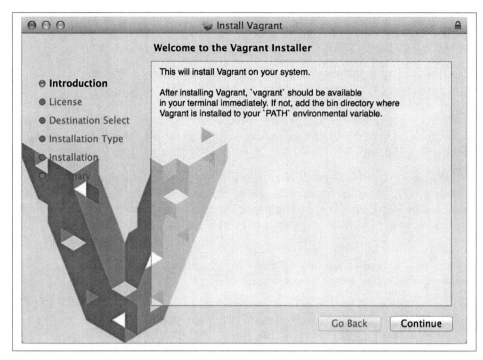

Figure 1-1. The Vagrant installer for Mac OS X

Figure 1-2. Verifying the installation worked on Mac OS X

Windows

For Windows, Vagrant is distributed as a standard MSI package. This means that once you're familiar with the manual installation process, Vagrant can also easily be added as an MSI package to be installed automatically across a fleet of computers if you're managing a large workgroup of Windows machines.

Find the Windows installer file from the downloads page opened previously, and download it to the computer you'd like to install Vagrant on.

The installer is a standard Windows installer in the format of an MSI. This is useful because while it is easy to install locally, Windows also provides many tools for remotely installing MSI-packaged software in case you're managing many machines. Installing Vagrant on remote Windows machines is outside the scope of this book, but searching for resources on remotely installing MSI packages should yield good results on how to do it.

Double-click the MSI and follow the instructions. The installer should look like Figure 1-3. You shouldn't have to modify any settings, but you can alter things like the installation directory if you'd like.

Figure 1-3. The Vagrant installer for Windows

As part of the installation process, the PATH environmental variable is modified to include the path to Vagrant. In order to see these changes, you'll have to restart any open command prompts. Vagrant is installed both as a batch file and as a bash file, so it's compatible with the Microsoft Command Prompt, PowerShell, and Cygwin.

To verify everything was installed correctly, open the command prompt of your choice and type vagrant --version. The output should include the Vagrant version you just installed. If you're still unsure, verify that the output looks similar to Figure 1-4.

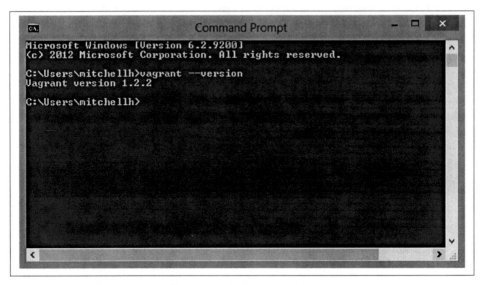

Figure 1-4. Verifying the installation worked on Windows

If everything looks good, then you're ready to rock!

Linux

For Linux, binary packages for many of the major distributions are available. If a compatible package is available for your distribution, download the package and follow the instructions for your package manager to install it.

If a package is unavailable for your distribution, you may fall back to the deprecated RubyGems installation method. You can report a bug to the project with your distribution and we'll do our best to provide a package. For more information on the RubyGem installation process, refer to the website. Since it is deprecated, it is not covered in this book.

For the Linux packages, Vagrant installs to */opt/vagrant*. You must add */opt/vagrant/bin* to your PATH manually in order to have access to the vagrant executable. Future packages will automatically create a symbolic link in */usr/bin* to avoid this extra step.

Once this is done, open up a terminal and type `vagrant --version` to verify Vagrant is available. The output should contain the version of Vagrant you just installed, and should look similar to the following output:

```
$ vagrant --version
Vagrant version 1.2.3
```

If everything looks good, then you're ready to go!

Common Mistakes

If installing Vagrant isn't working as expected, you should double-check to make sure that you haven'tmade one of the following common mistakes.

Improper PATH Configuration

First, make sure `vagrant` is configured to be accessible from the PATH variable. On Linux and Mac OS X, you can do this by typing `which vagrant` into your terminal. This should tell you where Vagrant is. If it doesn't, then Vagrant isn't on your path. On Linux, add */opt/vagrant/bin* to the path. On Mac OS X, add */Applications/Vagrant/bin* to the path.

On Windows, you can open the command prompt of your choice and type `where vagrant` to find out if Vagrant is on your path. If this tells you Vagrant was not found, then add *C:\vagrant\bin* to your path (note that if you chose to install it to another directory, you should use that directory).

Also, some installations of Windows, depending on their configuration, require a system restart to see `vagrant` on the path, so you should attempt that as well.

Conflicting RubyGems Installation

If Vagrant is on your path, but you're getting errors, then you should verify that you haven't previously installed Vagrant with RubyGems. If you have, use `gem uninstall vagrant` to remove it (the command may require administrative privileges), because it sometimes conflicts with the package-installed version.

Once Vagrant is uninstalled from RubyGems, reinstall Vagrant using the package. This must be done to ensure that Vagrant is properly added to your PATH.

If this wasn't helpful, use one of the Vagrant support channels covered in the next section to get help.

Using Vagrant Without VirtualBox

Since Vagrant 1.1, Vagrant has severed all ties that force you to use VirtualBox. Vagrant can now be used with VMware, EC2, and anything else you can dream of.

In Vagrant terminology, these are called "providers," and for this book, we will only use the VirtualBox provider. VirtualBox is free and works on every major platform that Vagrant runs on, so this is the lowest barrier to entry to using Vagrant.

However, once you learn more about Vagrant, if you prefer to use something other than VirtualBox, rest assured there are other options available. The creators of Vagrant offer an official VMware provider (*http://www.vagrantup.com/vmware*).

The examples in this book are tailored to VirtualBox, so I recommend using VirtualBox throughout the book.

Help!

If at any point in the book you're having problems or something is unclear, there are multiple resources available to receive help.

First, Vagrant's documentation site (*http://docs.vagrantup.com/*) is full of information that is constantly updated to cover new issues or difficulties people are facing. The documentation is also intuitively organized, so it should be easy to find the topic you need help with to see if the explanation there helps you to better understand.

Vagrant also has a strong community behind it (*http://www.vagrantup.com/support/ community.html*) made up of thousands of individuals using Vagrant in their own way. This community is very friendly and welcoming, and can be reached via the mailing list or IRC. It generally takes longer to get a response through the mailing list, but messages are seen by more eyes. With IRC, the chat is in real time, but someone with the right knowledge set or experience may not be available at the time a question is asked.

Finally, in addition to all these resources where you can reach an actual human, you can append --help to any Vagrant command and Vagrant will output help relevant to the command you're running. How this works will become clear as you progress through the book and become familiar with the Vagrant command-line tool.

CHAPTER 2

Your First Vagrant Machine

With Vagrant now installed on your system, let's create your first Vagrant-managed work environment. This chapter introduces the few components involved in using Vagrant. You'll see firsthand how easy it is to get started with Vagrant, how Vagrant can improve your workflow, and how fun having disposable work environments can be.

Vagrant is highly configurable—almost every default can be overridden. In this chapter, we'll use the defaults so you can see just how easy it is to get started with Vagrant. In subsequent chapters, we'll dive in depth into every feature exposed by Vagrant, so that you can make the perfect development environment.

To follow along in this chapter (and all remaining chapters in this book), you'll need to open a command-line interface (e.g., Terminal or the Windows Command Prompt) and a text editor (e.g., Emacs, Vim, Eclipse, TextMate, etc.).

Up and Running

You can get started by simply running the following two commands. This will involve Vagrant downloading a file that is around 300 MB, but it will save time later since we'll continue to reuse this file. The first command is the following:

```
$ vagrant init precise64 http://files.vagrantup.com/precise64.box
A `Vagrantfile` has been placed in this directory. You are now
ready to `vagrant up` your first virtual environment! Please read
the comments in the Vagrantfile as well as documentation on
`vagrantup.com` for more information on using Vagrant.
```

As the output indicates, you're now ready to run the second command `vagrant up`, which will generate the following:

```
$ vagrant up
Bringing machine 'default' up with 'virtualbox' provider...
[default] Box 'precise64' was not found. Fetching box from specified URL for
the provider 'virtualbox'. Note that if the URL does not have
a box for this provider, you should interrupt Vagrant now and add
the box yourself. Otherwise Vagrant will attempt to download the
full box prior to discovering this error.
Downloading with Vagrant::Downloaders::HTTP...
Downloading box: http://files.vagrantup.com/precise64.box
Extracting box...
Cleaning up downloaded box...
Successfully added box 'precise64' with provider 'virtualbox'!
[default] Importing base box 'precise64'...
[default] Matching MAC address for NAT networking...
[default] Setting the name of the VM...
[default] Clearing any previously set forwarded ports...
[default] Fixed port collision for 22 => 2222. Now on port 2200.
[default] Creating shared folders metadata...
[default] Clearing any previously set network interfaces...
[default] Preparing network interfaces based on configuration...
[default] Forwarding ports...
[default] -- 22 => 2200 (adapter 1)
[default] Booting VM...
[default] Waiting for VM to boot. This can take a few minutes.
[default] VM booted and ready for use!
[default] Configuring and enabling network interfaces...
[default] Mounting shared folders...
[default] -- /vagrant
```

After these commands finish running, an isolated, fully featured 64-bit Ubuntu 12.04 LTS virtual machine will be running in the background. It can't get much easier than that!

Don't believe me? Run vagrant ssh and you'll be dropped into a full-fledged SSH console within the virtual machine. You can do anything you'd like here, such as installing software, modifying files, or even removing the entire filesystem. The workflow and output of this is shown here:

```
$ vagrant ssh
Welcome to Ubuntu 12.04 LTS (GNU/Linux 3.2.0-23-generic x86_64)

 * Documentation:  https://help.ubuntu.com/
Welcome to your Vagrant-built virtual machine.
Last login: Fri Sep 14 06:23:18 2012 from 10.0.2.2
vagrant@precise64:~$
```

When you're done playing around with the SSH session, log out by typing exit and pressing enter. This will put you back into your terminal on the host machine.

Run vagrant destroy, and the virtual machine will be deleted and any resources it consumed such as RAM or disk space will be reclaimed:

```
$ vagrant destroy
Are you sure you want to destroy the 'default' VM? [y/N] y
[default] Forcing shutdown of VM...
[default] Destroying VM and associated drives...
```

Now that you know how easy it is to get started with Vagrant, let's take a slightly closer look at the pieces involved in using Vagrant.

The Vagrantfile

Vagrant is configured *per project*, where each project has its own isolated work environment. A project is denoted by the existence of a file named "Vagrantfile." Each project has a single Vagrantfile.

The Vagrantfile is a simple text file that Vagrant reads in order to determine what needs to be done to create your working environment. The file is a description of what operating system you want to boot, physical properties of the machine you need (e.g., RAM), what software needs to be installed on the machine, and various ways you'd like to access the machine over the network.

This file is meant to be placed under version control. Then, when another member of your team checks out the source of your project, they can use Vagrant to automatically and easily create their work environment without having to configure anything. With this practice, there is a small up-front cost of setting up the Vagrantfile, but then every member of your team benefits from Vagrant without any additional work.

Vagrantfiles are generally rarely modified, since the underlying settings of the development environment remain relatively stable compared to the actual codebase of the software being developed. Therefore, the majority of the price is truly paid up front. As iterations are made on the development environments, only minor changes need to be made to the Vagrantfile.

Yet, despite this initial up-front cost, Vagrant quickly makes up for the time spent in the stability and flexibility of the development environments it is able to automatically create. This is described in more detail in "The Tao of Vagrant" on page 4.

Now, let's create a Vagrantfile. In your terminal, create a folder to be your project directory for the duration of this book and navigate to that folder. On Linux and Mac OS X, it looks like this:

```
$ mkdir vagrant_book_example
$ cd vagrant_book_example
```

Once in the project directory, we can ask Vagrant to create an initial Vagrantfile by running `vagrant init` (as you've probably noticed, the `vagrant` command is used in combination with a handful of subcommands—e.g., `init`)—to control Vagrant):

```
$ vagrant init precise64 http://files.vagrantup.com/precise64.box
```

This is the first command that was run in "Up and Running" on page 15. After this, the directory the command was run in should contain a Vagrantfile. You can read the Vagrantfile if you'd like. It is heavily commented with examples and very basic documentation. This Vagrantfile is preconfigured and ready to be used, no additional modifications are necessary at this point.

The parameters given to the `vagrant init` command configure the "box" and "box_url" parameters within the Vagrantfile. You should see the values properly prefilled within the Vagrantfile. We'll cover what these mean exactly in the next section.

You may have noticed the file is not regular plain text. In fact, the Vagrantfile is written in a programming language named Ruby. If you don't know Ruby, that is OK! Most users of Vagrant are not Ruby programmers, and by following existing examples, you'll be able to configure every aspect of Vagrant without ever learning Ruby. Of course, if you do know Ruby, you can use your know-how to modify the Vagrantfile as you see fit. This can sometimes be convenient for more advanced configurations, but is rarely necessary.

Let's take a look at the structure of a very basic Vagrantfile. At its core, a Vagrantfile looks like the following (the functionality of each line will be covered later, so for this example, just the syntax will be explained):

```
Vagrant::Config.run do |config|    ❶
  config.vm.box = "precise64"    ❷

  config.vm.share_folder "v-root", "/vagrant", "."    ❸

  config.vm.provision "shell" do |s|    ❹
    s.path = "script.sh"
  end
end    ❺
```

❶ The first line starts a block of Vagrant configuration. The exact meaning of each part is unimportant. The `|config|` portion of the line says that for the duration of the configuration block, the configuration can be set on the `config` variable.

❷ The second line sets a basic configuration value for `config.vm.box` using simple variable assignment.

❸ The next line shows a config directive that isn't basic variable assignment. In this case, `share_folder` is a function call and three parameters are passed to it.

❹ This is also a functional call, this time to `provision`, but an additional configuration block is opened here, again using do and end. This pattern of opening configuration blocks is used throughout Vagrant configuration.

❺ The final line closes the configuration block opened on the first line.

And that's all there is to configuring Vagrant. No Ruby-specific knowledge is necessary, since the Vagrantfile is composed only of variable assignment, function calls, and configuration blocks.

Vagrantfiles are portable, meaning they can be read and used on every platform that Vagrant supports (Linux, Mac OS X, and Windows). This further simplifies setting up development environments, since once the Vagrantfile is set up, it can be used across a wide variety of operating systems, allowing your team members to use whatever system they feel most comfortable with.

V1 versus V2 Configuration

Vagrant supports two versions of configuration, known as V1 and V2 configuration.

V1 configuration is the configuration syntax from Vagrant 1.0.x, the first stable release of Vagrant. Vagrant promises backward compatibility of stable release configurations, so this syntax is still fully supported.

V2 configuration is the configuration syntax for what will become Vagrant 2.0, which is not yet released. The V2 configuration is experimental and actively changing while development toward 2.0 is done.

Because V2 is not yet stable, V1 configuration will be used throughout this book. If you attempt to put some of the configuration examples into a V2 block, you may see unexpected errors. You can verify that you're using V1 configuration because the Vagrantfile should start the configuration with Vagrant::Config.run. The overall structure of your Vagrantfile should be the following:

```
Vagrant::Config.run do |config|
  # ... configuration here
end
```

An important point is that as you learn more about Vagrant, you may encounter V2 configuration examples out in the wild. You can mix and match V1 and V2 configurations within the same Vagrantfile, so you can continue to leverage the knowledge gained in this book with new features that V2 may bring. For example, a Vagrantfile with the following structure is perfectly acceptable:

```
Vagrant::Config.run do |config|
  # V1 config here
end

Vagrant.configure("2") do |config|
  # V2 config here
end
```

Despite not using the latest configuration format, the knowledge in this book will easily transfer over when version 2 is stable.

Boxes

In addition to the Vagrantfile, Vagrant requires just one more thing before it can bring up the virtual machine: a box.

Because building a virtual machine from scratch is a resource-intensive and time-consuming endeavor, Vagrant uses a base image and clones it to rapidly create a usable machine. In Vagrant terminology, this base image is called a box and is distributed in the form of box files. An analogy that often helps people understand the purpose of box files is that box files are a template for a Vagrant-managed machine created later.

Boxes contain already-installed operating systems, so they're usually quite large, ranging from a few hundred megabytes to a few gigabytes. The 300 MB file downloaded in the earlier example was this box file. Luckily, Vagrant will save this box file for future usage, so it won't have to be downloaded again.

The box required is specified on a per-project basis via `config.vm.box` in the Vagrantfile. In our Vagrantfile, this was set to "precise64," the box requested from the call to `vagrant init`. Removing comments, the relevant Vagrantfile sections look like this:

```
Vagrant::Config.run do |config|
  config.vm.box = "precise64"
  config.vm.box_url = "http://files.vagrantup.com/precise64.box"
end
```

The value of `config.vm.box` specifies the name of the box. The box name maps to an installed box on the system. You'll see how boxes are managed later in Chapter 6. Multiple Vagrant environments can have the same `config.vm.box` value, and each environment will use the same underlying template when the machine is created.

We also set an optional configuration option `config.vm.box_url`. This option tells Vagrant where to find the necessary box if it isn't already available on the user's system. If you followed along with the example in "Up and Running" on page 15, you already saw Vagrant do this.

Multiple Vagrant environments often share the same underlying box, so Vagrant manages boxes globally, unlike Vagrantfiles, which are managed on a per-project basis. Once a box is downloaded, it can be used by multiple projects. Because Vagrant only uses the boxes as a base image to clone from, there is never any risk of conflicting changes. File modifications in one Vagrant environment never affect another.

The format of boxes and details on how to create new boxes will be covered in "Box Format" on page 74. For now, we'll use prebuilt boxes to learn the ins and outs of Vagrant. The box we chose earlier, "precise64," is a bare-bones 64-bit Ubuntu 12.04 LTS image.

Boxes are managed using the `vagrant box` command. Instead of using a URL in a Vagrantfile, boxes can also be added external to a project using `vagrant box add`.

Vagrant will list out the boxes that are installed using `vagrant box list`. And if you don't plan on using a box anymore, or want to replace a box, you can remove a box using `vagrant box remove`.

If a Vagrant project that uses a removed box is already running, it will not be affected, since Vagrant already cloned the box for that machine. However, projects that aren't running will need to re-download the box before they can be started.

Up

With a box configured and a Vagrantfile created, it is time to build the Vagrant environment, which can be accomplished by simply running `vagrant up`. You'll see the following output:

```
$ vagrant up
Bringing machine 'default' up with 'virtualbox' provider...
[default] Importing base box 'precise64'... ❶
[default] Matching MAC address for NAT networking... ❷
[default] Setting the name of the VM... ❸
[default] Clearing any previously set forwarded ports... ❹
[default] Creating shared folders metadata... ❺
[default] Clearing any previously set network interfaces... ❻
[default] Preparing network interfaces based on configuration...
[default] Forwarding ports... ❼
[default] -- 22 => 2222 (adapter 1)
[default] Booting VM... ❽
[default] Waiting for VM to boot. This can take a few minutes.
[default] VM booted and ready for use!
[default] Configuring and enabling network interfaces... ❾
[default] Mounting shared folders... ❿
[default] -- /vagrant
```

The command should take around 30 seconds to a minute to run, since the box was already downloaded in "Up and Running" on page 15. After it completes, an automatically created, fully self-contained VirtualBox virtual machine running Ubuntu 12.04 LTS will be running.

And that is the core power of Vagrant. The members of your team just need to know that a fully prepared development environment is only a `vagrant up` away, just as "The Tao of Vagrant" on page 4 states.

After a `vagrant up`, you won't see anything since Vagrant runs the virtual machines headless (without a graphical user interface) by default. But if you look at the running processes on your machine, you should see a `VBoxHeadless` process running. This is your virtual machine. In the next section, we'll show you how to access and manage this virtual machine.

Here's an explanation of each individual step to help you better understand what Vagrant is actually doing behind the scenes:

❶ During this step, Vagrant creates a new VirtualBox machine based on the base image within the box specified in the Vagrantfile. This process involves copying large virtual hard disk files and therefore can take some time.

❷ Most operating systems associate network configurations with the MAC address of their network devices. VirtualBox randomly generates a MAC address when creating a new machine. In order for the Internet access to work properly in the guest, Vagrant must set the MAC address of the network devices to be what they were when the operating system was installed. This information is retrieved from the box as well.

❸ This step sets the visible name of the virtual machine that you see if you open the VirtualBox application. When importing a machine, by default VirtualBox generates a random, unhelpful name. Vagrant by default sets the name to the name of the project directory with a timestamp attached to it. This helps identify virtual machines more easily. Of course, this can be further customized to whatever you'd like.

❹ Vagrant manages all forwarded port definitions, so it clears out any existing forwarded ports on the machine prior to setting its own. We haven't covered forwarded port definitions, but when we do, you'll understand the necessity of this step.

❺ VirtualBox requires the metadata about shared folders to be created prior to booting the machine. In this step, Vagrant configures the virtual machine with the shared folders that it will need.

❻ Vagrant also manages all the network interfaces on the virtual machine, so it first clears them, and then sets them up. At this point, we haven't covered how networking is done with Vagrant, so the details aren't important. However, when networking is covered later, this is the step where Vagrant prepares the actual virtual network devices.

❼ This step creates the metadata for the forwarded ports that VirtualBox will need. Forwarded ports are used for basic network access and most importantly for SSH later.

❽ Finally, after much preparation, Vagrant boots the machine. It then waits for the machine to complete booting, which is signaled by SSH becoming available.

❾ While a previous step prepared the metadata for the network devices, this step performs the actual operating system configuration for the network devices. Vagrant comes with deep knowledge of many operating systems, such as Ubuntu, RedHat, CentOS, FreeBSD, and many more. It uses this knowledge to properly configure networks based on the operating system you're using within the virtual machine.

❿ This step mounts shared folders so that data can be shared across the virtual machine and your host machine. This will be covered more in depth shortly.

All that is done automatically by Vagrant with just a couple lines of configuration. As you'll see later, with just a few additional lines of configuration, Vagrant can do much more. Furthermore, Vagrant does this across platforms on Mac OS X, Windows, and Linux.

Although it isn't covered in this book (since the feature is still being rapidly developed and iterated on), newer versions of Vagrant can take the same configuration and bring up machines in VMware, AWS, and other providers with little to no change to the configuration, and with an identical vagrant up. The flexibility is truly powerful.

Version Control and .vagrant/

As part of the vagrant up process, Vagrant creates a directory named *.vagrant/* in your project directory that is used to maintain some state for Vagrant.

This directory keeps track of guest machine IDs, locks, configurations, and more.

This state is specific to each vagrant up call, so the *.vagrant/* directory should be ignored by your version control system. Committing it into version control can cause Vagrant virtual machines to get "lost" or corrupted if they're accidentally shared.

Working with the Vagrant Machine

With the Vagrant environment created, it is time to learn how to use it. This section covers inspecting the state of the machine, accessing the machine, sharing files with the machine, communicating with the machine over the network, and tearing down and rebuilding the machine automatically.

Vagrant has a relatively small core set of commands available via the vagrant command. This makes it easy to learn and teach Vagrant. This follows the principles laid out in "The Tao of Vagrant" on page 4, keeping things simple to be minimally invasive on previous workflows.

State of the Vagrant Machine

Because Vagrant runs the virtual machines without a user interface, it is easy to forget the current state of the environment is (i.e., whether the virtual machine was created, if it's running, etc.). For this, `vagrant status` comes in handy:

```
$ vagrant status
Current machine states:

default                 running (virtualbox)

The VM is running. To stop this VM, you can run `vagrant halt` to
shut it down forcefully, or you can run `vagrant suspend` to simply
suspend the virtual machine. In either case, to restart it again,
simply run `vagrant up`.
```

As you can see, Vagrant tells us the machine is running. It also outputs some helpful information about what we can do with the machine in this state. If at any time you're unsure of what state your Vagrant environment is in, or how to move to another state, use `vagrant status`.

SSH

Accessing the machine is done via SSH. Vagrant includes the command `vagrant ssh`, which handles connecting and authenticating SSH, and drops you directly into an SSH prompt for the machine:

```
$ vagrant ssh
Welcome to Ubuntu 12.04 LTS (GNU/Linux 3.2.0-23-generic x86_64)

 * Documentation:  https://help.ubuntu.com/
Welcome to your Vagrant-built virtual machine.
Last login: Fri Sep 14 06:23:18 2012 from 10.0.2.2
vagrant@precise64:~$
```

This is a full-fledged SSH prompt inside a completely sandboxed virtual machine. You can do anything you want (e.g., install software, modify files, delete the entire filesystem, etc.). If you mess up your virtual machine, you can always re-create it, as we'll show in a few sections.

 SSH on Windows requires OpenSSH to be installed. It is left up to the reader to obtain this external software package. The easiest way to get this, however, is to set up Cygwin (*http://cygwin.com/*) or an MSYS environment such as msysgit (*https://code.google.com/p/msysgit/*).

If OpenSSH isn't available, Vagrant will output information on how to configure an SSH client such as PuTTY (*http://www.putty.org/*) to connect to the Vagrant machine.

Shared Filesystem

Vagrant supports setting up shared folders so that files and folders are synced to and from the virtual machine and the host machine. Having a shared filesystem between the host machine and the guest has numerous benefits.

First, and most important to developers using Vagrant, shared folders let users of Vagrant edit files using their own editor on the host machine, and have these changes synced into the virtual machine automatically. This is an important part of "The Tao of Vagrant" on page 4, because it doesn't impede on years of experience that developers may have with their particular toolsets.

The shared filesystem also gives you a place to store files that won't be destroyed as part of a vagrant destroy. When a guest machine is destroyed, files stored on the shared system are not deleted, and are therefore available the next time a machine is created with vagrant up, as long as the shared filesystem mapping is kept in the Vagrantfile.

Files on the shared filesystem are also ideal for files you may want to backup as part of routing system backups on the host system. Because virtual machine hard disks are large and giant binary blobs, they are usually ignored by host backup systems. Shared filesystems, on the other hand, just show up as a normal folder on the host, and are therefore more easily backed up. This is very useful for sensitive data you create from the guest machine that you may want backed up in the case of a disaster.

By default, Vagrant shares the project directory (the directory with the Vagrantfile) to */vagrant* inside the virtual machine. After SSHing into the virtual machine, this can be verified by listing the files in that directory:

```
vagrant@precise64:~$ ls /vagrant/
Vagrantfile
```

The Vagrantfile in that directory is actually the Vagrantfile from the project directory. If a file is created on the host machine or within the Vagrant machine, the changes will be mirrored from host to guest and vice versa.

The location of the default shared folder can be overridden from the Vagrantfile:

```
Vagrant::Config.run do |config|
  # …

  config.vm.share_folder "v-root", "/foo", "."
end
```

The config.vm.share_folder directive defines a shared folder for Vagrant. It takes a few parameters:

- First, an identifier for the shared folder. In this case, by specifying v-root, the default shared folder that Vagrant sets up is overridden.

- Next, */foo* is the path where the folder will exist in the guest machine. This path will be created if it doesn't already exist. If it does already exist, the location will be replaced with the contents of the shared folder.
- The third parameter, "." is the path of the folder to be shared from the host machine. This can be an absolute or relative path. If it is relative, like the example, it is relative to the project root. So in the example, it is sharing the project root.

For Vagrant to reconfigure the guest machine, the `vagrant reload` command must be run. This halts the machine, and then starts the machine again with the new configuration. It skips the initial step to clone the box, since the machine is already created. Your files and changes within the virtual machine are preserved.

Once the machine reboots, SSH in and you should see that the */foo* directory is now shared with the project root directory.

In addition to overriding the default shared folder, new shared folders can be defined as well. This looks very similar to what was done above, except now the first parameter should be a new, unique identifier for the shared folder:

```
Vagrant::Config.run do |config|
  # …

  config.vm.share_folder "data", "/data", "./data"
end
```

After another `vagrant reload`, the virtual machine will have a */data* directory synced with the *./data* directory on the host machine. This is in addition to the default shared folder setup.

Shared folders incur a heavy performance penalty within the virtual machine when there is heavy I/O, so they should only be used for source files. Any compilation step, database files, and so on should be done outside the shared folder filesystem inside the guest filesystem itself.

Basic Networking

Equally important as shared folders, Vagrant automatically configures various options for networking with the virtual machine. This allows developers using Vagrant to communicate with the machine.

This feature is import for environments such as web projects, because developers can continue using their own browser and development tools to access their project, while the web application code itself and all of its dependencies run isolated within the virtual machine. This is again an important aspect of "The Tao of Vagrant" on page 4.

All available networking options and their pros and cons will be explained in detail in Chapter 4. However, this section gives a quick example to show you the basics. To do this, we'll use a simple forwarded port. A forwarded port exposes a port on the guest machine as a port on the host machine. Let's expose port 80, so that we can access any web service. Modify the Vagrantfile to look like the following:

```
Vagrant::Config.run do |config|
  # …

  config.vm.forward_port 80, 8080
end
```

The config.vm.forward_port directive in the Vagrantfile defines a new forwarded port. In this case, Vagrant will forward port 80 on the guest to port 8080 on the host. Run vagrant reload to bring in the new changes.

```
$ vagrant reload
[default] Attempting graceful shutdown of VM...
[default] Setting the name of the VM...
[default] Clearing any previously set forwarded ports...
[default] Fixed port collision for 22 => 2222. Now on port 2200.
[default] Creating shared folders metadata...
[default] Clearing any previously set network interfaces...
[default] Preparing network interfaces based on configuration...
[default] Forwarding ports...
[default] -- 22 => 2200 (adapter 1)
[default] -- 80 => 8080 (adapter 1)
[default] Booting VM...
[default] Waiting for VM to boot. This can take a few minutes.
[default] VM booted and ready for use!
[default] Configuring and enabling network interfaces...
[default] Mounting shared folders...
[default] -- /vagrant
```

During the reload, notice that Vagrant forwarded the requested port.

To show that this forwarded port works, we'll start a simple web server from within the virtual machine and access it from a browser on the host machine:

```
$ vagrant ssh
vagrant@precise64:~$ cd /vagrant
vagrant@precise64:/vagrant$ sudo python -m SimpleHTTPServer 80
Serving HTTP on 0.0.0.0 port 80 ...
```

This uses a convenient command-line one-liner using Python to start a web server on port 80. Open a browser to *localhost:8080* on the host machine, and a directory listing of */vagrant*, served from the guest machine, will be shown, as in Figure 2-1.

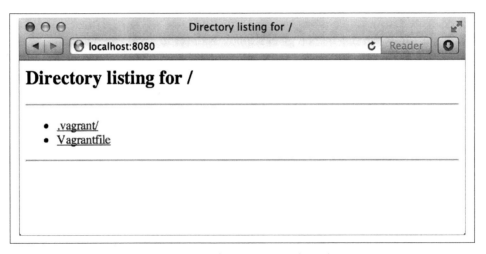

Figure 2-1. Viewing a web page served from the virtual machine

Forwarded ports are just one option available for networking with Vagrant. Additional options, their pros and cons, and the large number of ways they can be configured, will be covered in Chapter 4.

With forwarded ports and shared folders, developers can continue to use the development tools they're most comfortable and efficient with. Using Vagrant doesn't mean sacrificing your favorite browser or IDE. This helps not only with productivity, but it also makes deploying Vagrant within your environment easier, since there is less pushback from existing developers.

Teardown

At this point, there is a fully running Vagrant-managed virtual machine—with shared folders and networks defined—ready for work. But now let's say it is time to switch gears, maybe work on another project, maybe go out to lunch, or maybe just time to go home. It is time to clean up the Vagrant environment to leave our computer in a pristine state.

For many web developers, teardown of Vagrant environments is very cool. All web developers have at some point has made the mistake of forgetting to turn off the web server, database, or background job runner (or something similar) before going home. With Vagrant, this is simply impossible. Because all the software related to development is isolated within a single virtual machine, by remembering to run a single command, Vagrant is able to properly clean up the host machine.

After tearing down the machine, development can always be resumed with a vagrant up at any time. This causes Vagrant to automatically re-create the entire development environment, and pushes forward the idea of "The Tao of Vagrant" on page 4.

Vagrant can suspend, halt, or destroy the guest machine. Each of these functions has its time and place. Try each method and choose the one that works best for you.

Suspend

Suspending the guest machine will save the current running state of the machine and stop it. The machine can then later be resumed from this exact suspended state.

Suspending is literally a point-in-time snapshot of the machine. When the machine is later resumed, it begins executing the exact instruction it was at when it was suspended. This is unlike actually shutting down the machine, where the operating system goes through an entire shutdown sequence. With suspending, it is more like freezing time.

The main benefit of suspending is that resuming your work is very fast, usually taking no more than 5 to 10 seconds. You also resume exactly where you left off. This means that any web services, databases, in-memory cache, and so on are all left intact. The actual act of suspending is fairly fast too, taking 5 to 20 seconds depending on the size of the guest machine's RAM and the speed of the host machine's local hard disk.

The downside is that the hard disk space taken up by the guest machine remains, and guest machines can often take up 2 GB of disk space or more. In addition to this, extra disk space is needed to store the entire contents of the guest machine's RAM so that it can be properly resumed. This means that for a guest machine with 1 GB of RAM, one extra gigabyte of disk space is needed to suspend it.

After suspending the guest machine, no more CPU or RAM resources are consumed on the host machine for the Vagrant environment, but disk space continues to be used.

Vagrant will suspend the machine using `vagrant suspend`. The state of the machine can be inspected with the status command:

```
$ vagrant suspend
[default] Saving VM state and suspending execution...

$ vagrant status
Current machine states:

default                 saved (virtualbox)

To resume this VM, simply run `vagrant up`.
```

Later, the machine can be resumed with `vagrant up` or `vagrant resume`. The difference between the two is that the latter command will show an error if the machine isn't suspended, whereas the former will do the proper boot sequence depending on the state of the machine, even if it isn't suspended:

```
$ vagrant up
Bringing machine 'default' up with 'virtualbox' provider...
[default] Resuming suspended VM...
[default] Booting VM...
[default] Waiting for VM to boot. This can take a few minutes.
[default] VM booted and ready for use!
```

Halt

Halting the guest machine will shut it down, like a normal computer. The machine can then later be resumed via a normal boot up process, as if hitting the power button.

When halting, Vagrant will first attempt to gracefully halt the machine. Vagrant does this by executing the proper commands to initiate a shutdown from within the guest machine, such as shutdown on Linux. This allows the guest to execute a proper shutdown sequence, cleaning up all resources and safely shutting down.

If Vagrant is unable to gracefully shut down the machine, it will forcefully shut it down. This is the equivalent of physically pulling the power on the machine. Vagrant will resort to this if it is unable to communicate with the guest or if the graceful shutdown sequence times out.

The benefit of halting the Vagrant environment is that the guest machine is preserved while taking up no runtime resources of the host machine, such as CPU or RAM. The disk of the guest machine is preserved. When resumed, the Vagrant environment will start cleanly but avoid the potentially time-consuming import step. Unlike suspending, the RAM is not preserved, since the machine was fully shut down, so when you begin working again, you'll have to make sure the necessary processes such as web servers and databases are started again.

The downside to halting, similar to suspending, is that the guest machine continues to consume hard drive space. Depending on the guest machine, this can range from only 2 GB to more than 10 GB.

Vagrant will halt the machine when vagrant halt is called. The state of the machine, as always, can be inspected using vagrant status:

```
$ vagrant halt
[default] Attempting graceful shutdown of VM...

$ vagrant status
Current machine states:

default                  poweroff (virtualbox)

The VM is powered off. To restart the VM, simply run `vagrant up`
```

If you're not interested in gracefully shutting down the machine, the --force flag can be passed to Vagrant to simply force halt the machine:

```
$ vagrant halt --force
[default] Forcing shutdown of VM...
```

Later, when you're ready to begin working again, `vagrant up` will boot up and reconfigure the Vagrant environment. Note in the next example that the import step is skipped because the machine already exists:

```
$ vagrant up
Bringing machine 'default' up with 'virtualbox' provider...
[default] Setting the name of the VM...
[default] Clearing any previously set forwarded ports...
[default] Creating shared folders metadata...
[default] Clearing any previously set network interfaces...
[default] Preparing network interfaces based on configuration...
[default] Forwarding ports...
[default] -- 22 => 2222 (adapter 1)
[default] -- 80 => 8080 (adapter 1)
[default] Booting VM...
[default] Waiting for VM to boot. This can take a few minutes.
[default] VM booted and ready for use!
[default] Configuring and enabling network interfaces...
[default] Mounting shared folders...
[default] -- /vagrant
```

Destroy

Destroying the guest machine will shut it down and remove all traces of it by deleting hard disks, state files, and so on. After destroying the guest machine, the host machine should be returned to a pristine state as if `vagrant up` was never called.

Destroying a machine will cause you to lose *any* changes made to the machine while it was running, including any files or folders created outside of shared folders.

The benefit of destroying is that the host system is left in a pristine state. No extra hard disk space is taken up and no guest-related processes are running to consume CPU and RAM. The computer is left in such a state that it appears as if Vagrant was never run.

The downside of a full destroy is that the subsequent `vagrant up` to begin working again requires a full import and configuration of the guest machine. This takes considerably longer than resuming from suspend or booting after a halt.

Vagrant will destroy the guest when `vagrant destroy` is called:

```
$ vagrant destroy
Are you sure you want to destroy the 'default' VM? [y/N] y
[default] Forcing shutdown of VM...
[default] Destroying VM and associated drives...
```

```
$ vagrant status
Current machine states:

default                  not created (virtualbox)

The environment has not yet been created. Run `vagrant up` to
create the environment. If a machine is not created, only the
default provider will be shown. So if a provider is not listed,
then the machine is not created for that environment.
```

vagrant destroy asks you to confirm prior to actually executing, since destroy actually deletes all the virtual hard drives (i.e., if you have any data that isn't in a shared folder, it'll be lost).

You can skip the confirmation dialog by passing the --force flag to destroy:

```
$ vagrant destroy --force
[default] Forcing shutdown of VM...
[default] Destroying VM and associated drives...
```

Later, when you're ready to work again, vagrant up will re-create the Vagrant environment.

```
$ vagrant up
Bringing machine 'default' up with 'virtualbox' provider...
[default] Importing base box 'precise64'...
[default] Matching MAC address for NAT networking...
[default] Setting the name of the VM...
[default] Clearing any previously set forwarded ports...
[default] Creating shared folders metadata...
[default] Clearing any previously set network interfaces...
[default] Preparing network interfaces based on configuration...
[default] Forwarding ports...
[default] -- 22 => 2222 (adapter 1)
[default] -- 80 => 8080 (adapter 1)
[default] Booting VM...
[default] Waiting for VM to boot. This can take a few minutes.
[default] VM booted and ready for use!
[default] Configuring and enabling network interfaces...
[default] Mounting shared folders...
[default] -- /vagrant
```

What's Next?

In this chapter, we showed that a bare-bones Vagrant environment can be brought up in just two commands with no additional configuration.

Then, we went over the basics of how to work with this virtual machine. You saw how vagrant ssh allows you access to a full shell within the guest machine without having to memorize and juggle confusing authentication information.

Shared folders were introduced so that users of the virtual machine can modify files within the safety and comfort of their own tools on the host and have the files mirrored directly into the guest. And basic networking was shown so that developers can communicate with services in the virtual machine over the network. This is especially useful for web development and Internet browsers.

Finally, we showed you how easy it is to tear down the Vagrant environment. Depending on the situation, Vagrant offers multiple options to tear down the environment. Suspending the guest should be done if you want to restart the guest at the exact point it was left off, and hard disk space usage on the host doesn't matter. The guest should be halted if you want to boot the machine cleanly the next time the environment needs to be started, and also when hard disk space usage on the host doesn't matter. And the guest should be destroyed when you want your system to be left in a pristine state, and don't mind the extra startup time of the Vagrant environment when it needs to be started again.

Given all these important concepts, at this point you're hopefully seeing what the workflow of Vagrant looks like and how it relates to "The Tao of Vagrant" on page 4. You should also be seeing a glimpse of the configurability and flexibility Vagrant exposes so that it only positively impacts your existing development practices, such as being able to continue using your own editor, browser, and so on.

Next, we're going to take a look at provisioning, so that we can install software on the guest machine automatically when the Vagrant environment is created. We'll then continue looking at more advanced features of Vagrant.

CHAPTER 3

Provisioning Your Vagrant VM

According to "The Tao of Vagrant" on page 4, a developer can simply run `vagrant up` and have a complete development environment ready to go. This means that all the necessary software for each project being developed should be installed on the guest. This can be done one of two ways: baking the software into the box itself, or automatically installing the software as part of the development environment creation process. Provisioning does the latter.

In practice, the base boxes used by Vagrant are usually quite bare. The base box this book has been using in examples so far is a bare-bones Ubuntu 12.04 LTS installation. Only the minimal amount of software required to make it function with Vagrant (e.g., SSH) is installed.

The problem of installing software on a booted system is known as provisioning, and is often the job of shell scripts, configuration management systems, or manual command-line entry.

Vagrant supports automated provisioning, and will run configured provisioners on every `vagrant up` so that the necessary software and configurations needed to run the project being developed in the Vagrant environment are all properly prepared.

Out of the box, Vagrant supports provisioning with shell scripts, Chef, or Puppet. Additional provisioners can be added via plug-ins if your organization requires it.

In this chapter, we'll set up Apache to serve static files from the Vagrant shared folder. In the previous chapter, we did this by manually running Python's `SimpleHTTPServer` module. Instead of requiring a manual command to run, we'll configure Apache to automatically start and serve the files from the shared folder. This will allow developers of our basic example to work completely in their host environment, without ever having to SSH into the guest machine.

After showing the Apache installation as an example, it should be clear how Vagrant provisioning can be extended to provide something more complicated such as a full LAMP stack.

Why Automated Provisioning?

Automated provisioning offers three main benefits: ease of use, repeatability, and improving parity between development and production.

Too many developers today manually set up servers, copying and pasting configuration from guides online into the terminal prompt of their newly created server.

The problem with this arises when a new server needs to be set up. The same guides need to be tracked down in an attempt to create another identical server. In practice, the server ends up slightly different, and these differences can cause huge issues down the road. Main pain points usually come in the form of configuration differences, leading to common problems such as file handles running out, databases being improperly tuned, and so on.

The issue is further exacerbated when development machines need to be set up. Historically, without Vagrant, developers may have had a giant README file with various platform-specific steps to set up the machine for development. In the worst case, developers simply installed software until the errors when running it went away. This quickly leads to bugs where developers say "but it worked on my machine!"

Vagrant, along with automated provisioning, has the ability to remove this entire class of problem.

Whether developing on Windows, Mac OS X, or Linux, Vagrant runs an identical operating system to run the code for the project. With automating provisioning, identically configured and installed software is guaranteed as well. This essentially guarantees that any bugs seen are reproducible by every developer, and that the bugs would surely also exist in production.

An additional benefit with Vagrant is that automated provisioning used for production can be adapted to work in development as well, since the same OS as production is being used within the guest machines. If your organization has an operations team, then a majority of the work is already done, and they just need to be involved in setting up the Vagrant environments. As an added benefit: Vagrant is fantastic for quickly testing infrastructure changes locally, so ops people will have something to be excited about.

The result of all this is that there is a definite upfront cost to initially configure the automated provisioning for Vagrant, but it's a big win in productivity amortized over time. And these benefits are realized more quickly the more team members use Vagrant.

Supported Provisioners

Out of the box, Vagrant supports provisioning from shell scripts, Chef, or Puppet. A common question from newcomers to Vagrant is asking which provisioner to use. Most generally have heard that tools like Chef or Puppet are the "right" way to do things, but are afraid of their complexity.

If your ultimate goal is to become comfortable with Chef, Puppet, or some other formal configuration management tool, then Vagrant provides an ideal learning environment to do so. The ability to quickly create and destroy local machines on the fly makes learning these tools as frictionless as it can get.

I recommend starting with shell scripts. Learning Vagrant and a formal configuration management tool at the same time can be confusing. Shell scripts, on the other hand, are easy to understand and easy to hack together, resulting in some more instant gratification while learning Vagrant. After becoming familiar with Vagrant itself, then learning a configuration management tool becomes much easier.

If you're unfamiliar with Chef or Puppet, this book will not attempt to introduce you to them. There are a variety of resources, both online documents and published books, to learn more about each respective tool.

Vagrant supports provisioning Chef via either Chef Solo or Chef Client. Chef Solo is primarily useful for small deployments and quickly testing cookbooks during development. Chef Client is useful if your organization already uses a Chef Server, and you want Vagrant to hook into that existing infrastructure. If a Chef Server is not already in place, it usually isn't worth doing so just for the purpose of setting up Vagrant.

For Puppet, Vagrant supports provisioning with both a master using the Puppet Agent, or masterless by running `puppet apply` against a manifest and set of modules. Just as with Chef, the masterless approach is better for when you're just getting started with Puppet, small deployments, and testing individual modules. Connecting to a Puppet Master is better if the master is already in place and you want Vagrant to provision using existing scripts.

In addition to the built-in provisioners, Vagrant can be extended using plug-ins to add additional provisioners. So if you use a custom system or another configuration management tool not supported by Vagrant, you can easily add support for this. Actually, it is likely that the Vagrant open source community has already made a plug-in for you. You can usually find plug-ins by using your favorite search engine. Plug-in development is covered in Chapter 7.

Manually Setting Up Apache

Before using a provisioner, we'll manually set up Apache by installing and configuring it over SSH. This is usually the first step involved before setting up any automation, because we need to be aware of what needs to be done before we can automate it!

First, set up a project directory and create a Vagrantfile that looks like the following. We'll be using most of the defaults, except we'll add port forwarding so we can browse the served files we set up:

```
Vagrant::Config.run do |config|
  config.vm.box = "precise64"
  config.vm.forward_port 80, 8080
end
```

With the Vagrantfile created, `vagrant up`!

```
$ vagrant up
Bringing machine 'default' up with 'virtualbox' provider...
[default] Importing base box 'precise64'...
[default] Matching MAC address for NAT networking...
[default] Setting the name of the VM...
[default] Clearing any previously set forwarded ports...
[default] Creating shared folders metadata...
[default] Clearing any previously set network interfaces...
[default] Preparing network interfaces based on configuration...
[default] Forwarding ports...
[default] -- 22 => 2222 (adapter 1)
[default] -- 80 => 8080 (adapter 1)
[default] Booting VM...
[default] Waiting for VM to boot. This can take a few minutes.
[default] VM booted and ready for use!
[default] Configuring and enabling network interfaces...
[default] Mounting shared folders...
[default] -- /vagrant
```

After the machine is up and running, we'll need to SSH in to install and configure the software within the machine. Run `vagrant ssh` to enter an SSH prompt.

The base box being used is an Ubuntu machine, so Apt is the package manager used to install software. In case you're unfamiliar with the Ubuntu ecosystem, each step will be explained.

First, `apt-get update` needs to be run. This downloads the latest index of available packages so that when we attempt to install something, the package manager can find the most up-to-date available package.

This command—and many that follow—need to be run with `sudo` because they require root privileges. `sudo` is a command that executes another command with superuser privileges.

Typically, sudo will ask you to enter a password in order to gain these privileges, but you'll notice in all of the examples that follow that sudo works without any confirmation. This is because the precise64 base box, and many publicly available Vagrant boxes, are configured so that the vagrant user doesn't need to enter a password for sudo:

```
vagrant@precise64:~$ sudo apt-get update
Ign http://security.ubuntu.com precise-security InRelease
Ign http://us.archive.ubuntu.com precise InRelease
Ign http://us.archive.ubuntu.com precise-updates InRelease
Ign http://us.archive.ubuntu.com precise-backports InRelease
Get:1 http://security.ubuntu.com precise-security Release.gpg [198 B]
Hit http://us.archive.ubuntu.com precise Release.gpg
Get:2 http://security.ubuntu.com precise-security Release [49.6 kB]
...
Hit http://us.archive.ubuntu.com precise-backports/restricted Translation-en
Get:59 http://us.archive.ubuntu.com precise-backports/universe Translation-en
[16.2 kB]
Fetched 3,546 kB in 3s (914 kB/s)
Reading package lists... Done
```

After updating the package index, let's install Apache. This is done using apt-get install, which searches for and installs the named package. Note that some details from your output may differ from that in this book, but as long as there are no error messages, Apache will be successfully installed.

```
vagrant@precise64:~$ sudo apt-get install apache2
Reading package lists... Done
Building dependency tree
Reading state information... Done
The following extra packages will be installed:
  apache2-mpm-worker apache2-utils apache2.2-bin apache2.2-common
  libapr1 libaprutil1 libaprutil1-dbd-sqlite3 libaprutil1-ldap
  ssl-cert
Suggested packages:
    www-browser apache2-doc apache2-suexec apache2-suexec-custom ufw openssl-
blacklist
The following NEW packages will be installed:
  apache2 apache2-mpm-worker apache2-utils apache2.2-bin apache2.2-common
  libapr1 libaprutil1 libaprutil1-dbd-sqlite3
  libaprutil1-ldap ssl-cert
0 upgraded, 10 newly installed, 0 to remove and 57 not upgraded.
Need to get 1,855 kB of archives.
After this operation, 5,679 kB of additional disk space will be used.
Do you want to continue [Y/n]? y
Get:1 http://us.archive.ubuntu.com/ubuntu/ precise/main libapr1 amd64 1.4.6-1
[89.6 kB]
...
Fetched 1,855 kB in 2s (728 kB/s)
Preconfiguring packages ...
Selecting previously unselected package libapr1.
(Reading database ... 23067 files and directories currently installed.)
```

```
Unpacking libapr1 (from .../libapr1_1.4.6-1_amd64.deb) ...
Selecting previously unselected package libaprutil1.
...
Processing triggers for ureadahead ...
ureadahead will be reprofiled on next reboot
...
Setting up apache2.2-bin (2.2.22-1ubuntu1.2) ...
Setting up apache2-utils (2.2.22-1ubuntu1.2) ...
Setting up apache2.2-common (2.2.22-1ubuntu1.2) ...
Enabling site default.
Setting up apache2-mpm-worker (2.2.22-1ubuntu1.2) ...
 * Starting web server apache2
apache2: Could not reliably determine the server's fully qualified domain name,
using 127.0.1.1 for ServerName
[ OK ]
Setting up apache2 (2.2.22-1ubuntu1.2) ...
Setting up ssl-cert (1.0.28ubuntu0.1) ...
Processing triggers for libc-bin ...
ldconfig deferred processing now taking place
```

By default, Ubuntu sets up Apache to start when the system boots, and Apache comes out of the box serving files from */var/www*. To make configuration simple, we're just going to change */var/www* to be a symbolic link to the default shared folder directory */vagrant*. This way, any files we put into the shared folder will be served from Apache by default, and we don't have to actually modify any Apache configuration files.

```
vagrant@precise64:~$ sudo rm -rf /var/www
vagrant@precise64:~$ sudo ln -fs /vagrant /var/www
```

If you visit *http://localhost:8080* now, you should see a directory listing of the shared folder. To prove it works, create an *index.html* file on the host, and refresh to view it in your browser. Exit SSH and create the index file:

```
vagrant@precise64:~$ logout
Connection to 127.0.0.1 closed.
$ echo "<strong>Hello!</strong>" > index.html
```

After the index file is created, refresh your browser and you should see the change, as shown in Figure 3-1.

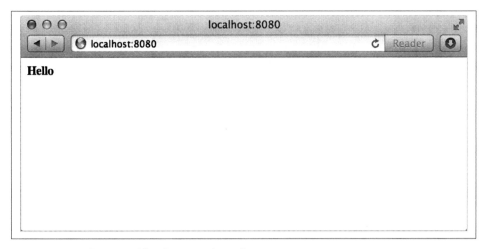

Figure 3-1. Index served by the virtual machine

Success! We can now make simple web pages on our own machine, using our own editor, and instantly refresh a web browser to view the web pages served from inside the virtual machine.

Imagine what a pain it would be doing this manual process every time `vagrant up` is run. It just shuffles the work of setting up development environments from your machine to a virtual machine. Regardless, this is an improvement thanks to the sandbox that virtual machines provide. But with automated provisioning, this pain goes away, and suddenly the setup of the development environment will become easily repeatable for other members of the team.

Automated Provisioner Basics

Now that we've gone through the process of setting up Apache manually, we're in a much better position to automate the whole process, since we know and understand the steps involved.

Before reviewing formal configuration management tools like Chef or Puppet, we'll first automate the process using shell scripts. If you're new to Chef or Puppet and plan on using either of those options instead, doing simple things with shell first and then converting it to Chef or Puppet can be a worthwhile exercise. So let's get started by creating a shell script to automatically set up Apache.

Shell Scripts

Shell scripts, at their most basic form, are just a list of commands to run. Therefore, we can make a simple shell script with the commands that we ran earlier, but in a file. Create the following *provision.sh* file in your project directory:

```
#!/usr/bin/env bash

echo "Installing Apache and setting it up..."
apt-get update >/dev/null 2>&1
apt-get install -y apache2 >/dev/null 2>&1
rm -rf /var/www
ln -fs /vagrant /var/www
```

The shell script has some minor differences from what we typed into the command line. First, the initial line is called a shebang and specifies what shell to use to execute the rest of the file. In this case, we're using bash.

Next, we echo to the user what will be done. We do this because we silence the remaining commands so that our terminal isn't filled with output.

Then we remove all the calls to `sudo`. Vagrant will run the script as root, so there is no need to actually use `sudo`.

Finally, there is a subtle change to installing Apache. If you didn't notice, the `-y` flag is now passed to install the Apache package. This flag tells `apt-get` to automatically respond "yes" to any prompts. Because `apt-get` usually asks for confirmation of whether we want to actually install the package or not, this will automatically say yes. This is important because for automated provisioning, there is no human interaction, so if `apt-get` were to ask for confirmation, the script would simply never finish, or crash.

With the shell script created, the next step is to configure Vagrant to use the script. Add the following line somewhere in the Vagrantfile:

```
config.vm.provision "shell", path: "provision.sh"
```

And that's it! This one line tells Vagrant to provision the machine with the shell provisioner, and to use the shell script at the path *provision.sh*. Relative paths (as opposed to full, absolute paths) are always relative to the project root.

Your full Vagrantfile might now look something like this:

```
Vagrant::Config.run do |config|
  config.vm.box = "precise64"
  config.vm.forward_port 80, 8080
  config.vm.provision "shell", path: "provision.sh"
end
```

Before running Vagrant to verify this worked, make sure you destroy the machine so that we can start from a clean state. Run `vagrant destroy`. If you didn't follow any of the preceding examples, then you may not have a machine running, in which case Vagrant will tell you so and no harm is done.

Finally, run `vagrant up`, and behold the beauty of automation. In the following output, some common elements you've seen over and over have been snipped out to make it easier to see the important details of what is going on:

```
$ vagrant up
Bringing machine 'default' up with 'virtualbox' provider...
[default] Importing base box 'precise64'...
...
[default] VM booted and ready for use!
[default] Configuring and enabling network interfaces...
[default] Mounting shared folders...
[default] -- /vagrant
[default] Running provisioner: VagrantPlugins::Shell::Provisioner...
stdin: is not a tty
Installing Apache and setting it up...
```

The whole `vagrant up` process might take a couple more minutes than usual this time since it has to provision the machine.

Once it completes, open your browser and visit *http://localhost:8080*. You should see the same web page that you saw when you manually set up Apache in the previous section. Without any human interaction (other than telling Vagrant to create the environment), a complete, very basic web development environment has been created.

It shouldn't be hard to mentally extrapolate what we've just done and imagine setting up much more complex environments. Imagine just running `vagrant up` and having a web server, database, background jobs, crons, and so on, all set up and ready to go for development. In fact, this is actually how Vagrant works in real-world situations. Every team member gets an automatically set up, identical, sandboxed development environment.

Chef

Chef is a configuration management framework built by Opscode, and is widely used by organizations large and small. A tutorial on Chef is outside the scope of this book, so this section is meant for people who are already comfortable with Chef or have a separate tutorial open and are using Vagrant at the same time.

Vagrant has built-in support for provisioning with Chef, using both `chef-solo` and `chef-client`. Chef Solo uses local cookbooks to provision the machine, whereas Chef Client connects to a Chef Server in order to download the cookbooks and run list. In this example, we're going to just use Chef Solo, since it is the easiest. Chef Server configurations are covered in "In-Depth Provisioner Usage" on page 48.

Before setting up the actual Chef cookbooks and recipes we'll need, let's configure the Vagrantfile. As with most things with Vagrant, it is extremely simple to get started with the Chef provisioner. Add the following line somewhere in your Vagrantfile:

```
config.vm.provision "chef_solo", run_list: ["vagrant_book"]
```

And that's it! In typical Vagrant fashion, there are some assumed defaults in this basic configuration. Most importantly, by default Vagrant will look for cookbooks in the *cookbooks* directory relative to the project directory.

Your full Vagrantfile might now look something like this:

```
Vagrant::Config.run do |config|
  config.vm.box = "precise64"
  config.vm.forward_port 80, 8080
  config.vm.provision "chef_solo", run_list: ["vagrant_book"]
end
```

Now let's create the actual cookbook and recipe. Save the following file to *cookbooks/vagrant_book/recipes/default.rb* relative to your project directory:

```
execute "apt-get update"
package "apache2"
execute "rm -rf /var/www"
link "/var/www" do
  to "/vagrant"
end
```

Since Chef knowledge is assumed, we won't go over how the recipe works, but it should be fairly obvious for someone who has used Chef that this recipe matches up with the manual steps we did previously.

At this point, the layout of your project directory should look something like the following:

```
$ tree
.
├── Vagrantfile
└── cookbooks
    └── vagrant_book
        └── recipes
            └── default.rb

3 directories, 2 files
```

We're ready to provision. Make sure that you vagrant destroy if there is a previous guest running so that we can start from a clean slate. Then, run vagrant up (again, only the relevant parts of the output are shown here; the rest have been clipped out):

```
$ vagrant up
Bringing machine 'default' up with 'virtualbox' provider...
[default] Importing base box 'precise64'...
...
```

```
[default] VM booted and ready for use!
[default] Configuring and enabling network interfaces...
[default] Mounting shared folders...
[default] -- /vagrant
[default] -- /tmp/vagrant-chef-1/chef-solo-1/cookbooks
[default] Running provisioner: VagrantPlugins::Chef::Provisioner::ChefSolo...
Generating chef JSON and uploading...
Running chef-solo...
stdin: is not a tty
[2013-03-25T23:47:05+00:00] INFO: *** Chef 10.14.2 ***
[2013-03-25T23:47:05+00:00] INFO: Setting the run_list to ["vagrant_book"] from
JSON
[2013-03-25T23:47:05+00:00] INFO: Run List is [recipe[vagrant_book]]
[2013-03-25T23:47:05+00:00] INFO: Run List expands to [vagrant_book]
[2013-03-25T23:47:05+00:00] INFO: Starting Chef Run for precise64
[2013-03-25T23:47:05+00:00] INFO: Running start handlers
[2013-03-25T23:47:05+00:00] INFO: Start handlers complete.
[2013-03-25T23:47:05+00:00] INFO: Processing execute[apt-get update] action run
    (vagrant_book::default line 1)
[2013-03-25T23:47:14+00:00] INFO: execute[apt-get update] ran successfully
[2013-03-25T23:47:14+00:00] INFO: Processing package[apache2] action install
    (vagrant_book::default line 2)
[2013-03-25T23:47:20+00:00] INFO: Processing execute[rm -rf /var/www] action run
    (vagrant_book::default line 3)
[2013-03-25T23:47:20+00:00] INFO: execute[rm -rf /var/www] ran successfully
[2013-03-25T23:47:20+00:00] INFO: Processing link[/var/www] action create
    (vagrant_book::default line 4)
[2013-03-25T23:47:20+00:00] INFO: link[/var/www] created
[2013-03-25T23:47:20+00:00] INFO: Chef Run complete in 14.234617 seconds
[2013-03-25T23:47:20+00:00] INFO: Running report handlers
[2013-03-25T23:47:20+00:00] INFO: Report handlers complete
```

Once it completes, open your browser and visit *http://localhost:8080*. You should see the same web page that you saw when you manually set up Apache in the previous section. Chef and Vagrant worked together to create a complete, basic web development environment without any human interaction other than telling Vagrant to "go!"

Puppet

Puppet is a configuration management framework built by PuppetLabs. It is used by thousands of companies large and small. A tutorial on Puppet is outside the scope of this book, so this section is meant for people who are already comfortable with Puppet or have a separate tutorial open and are using Vagrant at the same time.

Vagrant has built-in support to provision with Puppet, either with or without a Puppet Master. In order to keep the example simple, this section will show you how to use Puppet without a master. This is also the best way to learn Puppet if you're just starting out, and is generally a prerequisite to using a master anyways.

First, let's configure Vagrant to use Puppet. This is a one-liner:

```
config.vm.provision "puppet"
```

As usual, Vagrant will make a lot of assumptions about how our Puppet manifests and such are laid out. All of these assumptions can be overridden but they're generally good practice so we're going to go with it.

By default, Vagrant expects manifests to be in the *manifests* folder, and will run the *default.pp* manifest in that folder to kick off the Puppet run.

Next, let's create the Puppet manifest that will set up our instance. Create the file *manifests/default.pp* relative to your project root with the following contents:

```
exec { "apt-get update":
  command => "/usr/bin/apt-get update",
}

package { "apache2":
  require => Exec["apt-get update"],
}

file { "/var/www":
  ensure => link,
  target => "/vagrant",
  force  => true,
}
```

For anyone who knows Puppet, the preceding manifest should be straightforward.

With this manifest in place, the layout of your project directory should look like the following:

```
$ tree
.
├── Vagrantfile
└── manifests
    └── default.pp

1 directories, 2 files
```

Now we're ready to run Puppet. Make sure you vagrant destroy if you have a previous guest running so that we start from a clean slate. Then, run vagrant up (again, only the relevant parts of the output are shown here):

```
$ vagrant up
Bringing machine 'default' up with 'virtualbox' provider...
[default] Importing base box 'precise64'...
...
[default] VM booted and ready for use!
[default] Configuring and enabling network interfaces...
[default] Mounting shared folders...
[default] -- /vagrant
[default] -- /tmp/vagrant-puppet/manifests
[default] Running provisioner: VagrantPlugins::Puppet::Provisioner::Puppet...
```

```
Running Puppet with default.pp...
stdin: is not a tty
notice: /Stage[main]//Exec[apt-get update]/returns: executed successfully
notice: /Stage[main]//Package[apache2]/ensure:  ensure  changed  'purged'  to
'present'
notice: /Stage[main]//File[/var/www]/ensure:  ensure  changed  'directory'  to
'link'
notice: Finished catalog run in 12.82 seconds
```

Once Vagrant finishes running, open your browser and visit *http://localhost:8080*. You should see the same web page you saw when you manually set up Apache in the previous section.

Puppet and Vagrant together have created a complete, basic web development environment without any human interaction other than telling Vagrant to "go!"

Multiple Provisioners

You aren't limited to using a single provisioner. By specifying multiple config.vm.pro vision directives in the Vagrantfile, Vagrant will provision the guest machine using each provisioner in the order they're specified.

You can specify as many different provisioners as you'd like, or use multiple of the same provision, which is sometimes useful for many shell scripts.

In practice, a Vagrantfile using multiple provisioners looks like the following:

```
Vagrant::Config.run do |config|
  config.vm.box = "precise64"

  config.vm.provision "shell", inline: "apt-get update"
  config.vm.provision "puppet"
  # ... and so on
end
```

After specifying multiple provisioners, you can even tell Vagrant to provision using only specific provisioners. As an example, this is useful when you may have a shell script to bootstrap the machine, and you're using the Chef provisioner to test Chef cookbooks and you only want to run the Chef provisioner during a reload. To both up and reload, you can do the following:

```
$ vagrant up --provision-with=chef
...
```

Of course, you can put the name of whatever provisioner you're using as a parameter here.

"No Provision" Mode

As your automated provisioning setup becomes more complex, the time it takes for the provisioners to run can quickly turn into many minutes. In these cases, it is sometimes nice to be able to tell Vagrant to temporarily disable provisioning.

This can be done with the `--no-provision` flag to `up` or `reload`:

```
$ vagrant up --no-provision
...
```

This flag is most commonly used with `reload` when new configuration may have been added to the Vagrantfile, but when you don't necessarily want to wait for all the provisioners to run again.

In-Depth Provisioner Usage

Now that you've seen the basics of how to use the automated provisioners, we'll go into gory details of how each provisioner can be configured and tuned to do exactly what you want.

This section is more useful as a reference, so feel free to skip it if you feel comfortable with just the basics. Otherwise, save time by just reading the section relevant to the automated provisioner you use.

Shell Scripts

Shell scripts are unique because they're flexible, ranging from extremely simple to incredibly complex. In this section, we show the features Vagrant offers to make working with shell scripts easier, or to achieve certain tasks with shell scripts in an idiomatic way.

Inline scripts

In the shell provisioner basics, a separate file was used for the shell script. Sometimes, what you want to do is so simple that creating another file seems like overkill. In these cases, you can specify an inline script:

```
config.vm.provision "shell", inline: "apt-get install -y apache"
```

By specifying an inline script, Vagrant will use the default shell and execute the given command. This is very handy for quick, one-off tasks with the shell provisioner.

Run-once scripts

One of the great features of formal configuration management systems is that they're idempotent, meaning they can be run many times but the end result remains the same. Shell scripts, on the other hand, aren't idempotent unless you manually specify them to be. And doing this is usually cumbersome.

As a trick, it is very common to see shell scripts turned into run-once scripts by using clever file existence checks. Here is an example shell script to do this:

```
if [ -f "/var/vagrant_provision" ]; then
  exit 0
fi

# Actual shell commands here.

touch /var/vagrant_provision
```

This is a simple solution to making your shell scripts run once, and is a commonly used pattern within the Vagrant community.

Chef Server

In addition to running Chef against local cookbooks, Vagrant supports provisioning the machine by using a remote Chef Server. The Chef Server determines the proper run list for the node and sends down the cookbooks to provision the machine.

If you're new to Chef, I recommend sticking with local Chef cookbooks. Provisioning Vagrant machines with a Chef Server is most useful for organizations and environments where the Chef infrastructure is already in place and you'd like to hook into that.

Taking advantage of preexisting Chef infrastructure at your organization is the best way to provision development environments as similar to production as possible. It also forces the Chef cookbooks to remain more stable in development as well as production, since they're actively being used in both environments.

Configuring Vagrant to provision by connecting to a Chef Server is simple:

```
config.vm.provision "chef_client",
  chef_server_url: "http://mychefserver.com:4000/",
  validation_key_path: "validation.pem"
```

Additional options are available if you need them to authenticate:

validation_client_name
  This is sometimes required when using the hosted Chef Server platform that Opscode provides.

client_key_path
  This should be used if you want the node to register using an existing client key.

In addition to these authentication options, you can also specify some configuration options. environment is the Chef environment you want to register the node in. Chef environments are a way for you to segment your cookbooks into environment-specific silos such as "development" or "staging."

As usual, running any Vagrant command that runs provisioners will provision the machine using the Chef Server.

 Vagrant does not automatically remove the node or client from the Chef Server when vagrant destroy is called. Because of this, you may run into "existing client" or 403 errors when attempting to run vagrant up again. You should make sure the hostname of the machine on every vagrant up is different, or find a plug-in to automatically unregister the node when vagrant destroy is called.

Puppet

Puppet is a mature, complex tool that supports a wide range of features. In the basic example shown previously, we only used the bare minimum set of features to get what we needed working. However, Vagrant supports easy configuration of many additional Puppet features. The following sections explain how to use specific features of Puppet with Vagrant, allowing you to more easily integrate an existing Puppet environment into Vagrant, or to use more features of Puppet if you're getting started.

Modules

In "Automated Provisioner Basics" on page 41, we just used a single Puppet manifest to provision the machine. In reality, Puppet code is typically broken down into a set of reusable components known as *modules* (*http://bit.ly/16EsTHj*).

The Puppet provisioner for Vagrant fully supports modules by specifying the module_path in the Vagrantfile:

```
config.vm.provision "puppet",
  module_path: "modules"
```

This is the path to the modules on the host filesystem. If the path is relative, it is expanded relative to the project root.

Vagrant will share or copy all the modules in this directory to the guest machine and configure Puppet properly so that Puppet is able to find these modules.

Once the module path is set up, you can include modules as usual in your manifest file, or from other modules using normal Puppet include or require syntax. For example, if you had an "apache2" Puppet module, the default manifest file could contain the following to install Apache:

```
include apache2
```

Hiera Data

Hiera (*http://docs.puppetlabs.com/hiera/latest/*) is a tool for configuration data within Puppet that allows you to easily set configuration values depending on system attributes without requiring complex conditionals within the Puppet code itself. For example, Hiera is good for setting a different variable value depending on if the system is a Linux or Windows machine.

Vagrant supports exposing Hiera configuration into your Puppet code as a simple configuration parameter:

```
config.vm.provision "puppet",
  hiera_config_path: "hiera.yaml"
```

The value of `hiera_config_path` is the path to the Hiera configuration file on the host system. If the path is relative, it is expanded relative to the project root.

Vagrant will share or copy that file into the guest machine and will configure Puppet so that it loads this file for Hiera configuration.

It is common for the Hiera configuration to specify the Hiera data directories using relative paths. These paths are relative to the working directory when Puppet is run. Because this is so common, there is an additional configuration parameter (`working_di rectory`) to specify the working directory when Puppet is run. In conjunction with `hiera_config_path`, this allows you to run Puppet against the Hiera setup you would use in production:

```
config.vm.provision "puppet",
  hiera_config_path: "hiera.yaml",
  working_directory: "/vagrant"
```

The `working_directory` variable specifies the path on the guest machine to use as the working directory, and must be an absolute path.

Custom Facts

Puppet brings in a set of variables with knowledge of the running system from Facter (*http://docs.puppetlabs.com/facter/*). The information available from Facter includes things like the operating system, network interface information, filesystem information, and so on. This auto-detected information (known as "facts") is available as top-level variables in Puppet.

Vagrant supports setting custom facts from the Vagrantfile:

```
config.vm.provision "puppet" do |p|
  p.facter["vagrant"] = "yes"
end
```

The `facter` configuration variable is available and can be set like a Ruby hash (key-value mapping). These mappings are then exposed as facts to the running Puppet system. The `facter` configuration variable must be set using the expanded provisioner configuration format, as just shown, rather than the shorthand, single-line approach.

Given the previous example, the `$vagrant` variable would be available and set within Puppet code with the value of "yes."

Custom facts from a Vagrantfile are useful for many reasons. One use case is demarcating a Puppet run within Vagrant. This allows you to perform custom logic or avoid certain tasks if Puppet is running within Vagrant. A common thing to avoid in Vagrant environments is setting up monitoring systems, since Vagrant environments are generally only for development and don't need robust monitoring systems.

Another popular use case is to simulate facts of another system to test how the Puppet code will behave. For example, perhaps the `$private_network` fact is set to true on production systems if the machine is booted on the private network. You can manually set this to true for Vagrant environments to test and verify that Puppet properly runs certain code paths.

Using a Puppet Master

In addition to running Puppet against local manifests and modules, Vagrant supports provisioning the machine by connecting to a remote Puppet Master. The Puppet Master determines the proper set of modules and manifests to run on the node, and sends it down to provision the machine.

If you're new to Puppet, I recommend sticking with local Puppet code. Provisioning Vagrant machines with a Puppet Master is most useful for organizations and environments where the Puppet infrastructure is already in place and you'd like to take advantage of that.

Configuring Vagrant to use an existing Puppet Master is the best way to provision development environments as similar as possible to production. It also forces the Puppet modules to remain more stable in development as well as production since they're actively being used in both environments.

Configuring Vagrant to provision using a Puppet Master couldn't be easier:

```
config.vm.provision "puppet_server"
```

That's it! As usual, this assumes many sane defaults that Vagrant sets. Without additional configuration, Puppet will look for the Puppet Master at the hostname "puppet" and will register itself with the hostname of the guest machine as the name of the Puppet node.

Of course, additional configuration options are available if you wish to customize this behavior:

`puppet_server`
> The hostname of the Puppet Master. It defaults to "puppet".

`puppet_node`
> The name of the node that the Puppet Agent will register itself as with the Puppet Master. This defaults to the hostname of the guest machine.

`facter`
> This can be used to set custom facts. See "Custom Facts" on page 51.

`options`
> This can be used to set a string or array of additional command-line options to pass to the `puppet` program. This is for advanced usage only, but is useful for setting custom flags or configuration values that Vagrant doesn't expose as higher level primitives.

Once the provisioner is configured in the Vagrantfile, running any Vagrant command that runs provisioners will provision the machine using a Puppet Master.

What's Next?

In this chapter, we introduced all the available automated provisioners in Vagrant, showing how they're used to set up a basic Apache web sever as an example.

Most importantly, you should now understand the importance of automated provisioning, especially for the Vagrant workflow. By embracing automated provisioning, development environment creation is repeatable and identical for every member of your team.

In addition to the basic examples, we covered some of the more advanced features of each provisioner, so that you can always refer back to this book as a reference for anything you may need to do with the provisioners.

Next, we're going to introduce all the available options for networking in Vagrant. We briefly introduced forwarded ports in Chapter 2, but Vagrant offers many more options with their own set of use cases so that you can work most effectively with the virtual machine.

CHAPTER 4

Networking in Vagrant

Part of the ideal Vagrant workflow is the firm belief that you should be able to continue using existing browsers and development tools on your local machine.

One example of this is shared folders, which you saw briefly when setting up your first Vagrant environment. Shared folders allow you to work on your own machine and have files synced into the guest machine, letting you continue to use your own editor.

Likewise, to use your own browser for web applications, we need a way to expose network applications such as web servers to the outside world from the virtual machine. To do this, Vagrant exposes a set of options for networking the virtual machine.

Vagrant offers three networking options to maximize flexibility: forwarded ports, host-only networking, and bridged networking.

Each networking option has its own specific use case and set of upsides and downsides. Understanding each of these is important to getting the most value possible from Vagrant.

For this chapter, we'll continue building on the previous virtual machine configured to install Apache. If you haven't done this yet, spend some time quickly setting up your Vagrantfile with the shell configuration to install Apache. If you're using Chef or Puppet, that is fine, as long as it is provisioned following the examples in Chapter 3.

Using this virtual machine running Apache, we'll review each option of networking in order to see how it works, and the benefits and costs associated with each.

Forwarded Ports

With forwarded ports, Vagrant will set up a port on the host to forward to a port on the guest, allowing you to access services on the guest without an IP.

We've been using forwarded ports already throughout this book, so the basics of this feature should not be new.

As an example, if you forwarded port 80 (the standard port for serving HTTP content) in the guest to port 8080 on your host, then you could access the web server in the guest by loading *localhost:8080* on your main machine. The traffic sent to port 8080 is actually forwarded to port 80 on the guest machine.

Pros and Cons

The benefits of forwarded ports is that they're very simple to set up. You just tell Vagrant in the Vagrantfile what ports to forward where.

The simplicity of forwarded ports comes at a cost. First, you need to be explicit about every port you want to forward. For basic web services, this is easy. But there are also databases, services that listen on multiple ports, and more that can be useful to access, and configuring all of this becomes tedious very quickly.

Forwarded ports are also accessible from outside your own computer. Assuming you don't have a firewall in place, any computer on the local network can access your virtual machine if they know your IP and the port that it is listening on. For local development this is often not a big issue, but it is worth noting for those who are more sensitive to security and privacy.

And finally, with VirtualBox, Vagrant can't forward to ports less than 1024 on the host system. This is due to operating systems not allowing this for processes without administrative privileges, such as Vagrant. The main use case this negatively affects is SSL, which is assumed to be on port 443 for web traffic. If you want to test SSL, port forwarding is not a good way to do it.

Basic Usage

We've been configuring forward ports throughout this book, so this shouldn't be new. It is very simple:

```
config.vm.forwarded_port 80, 8080
```

The first argument is the port on the guest to make available via the host port, which is the second argument.

Multiple forwarded port definitions can be included in a Vagrantfile in order to forward multiple ports.

Just like any other configuration change in Vagrant, these changes won't take effect on running machines until a vagrant reload is called.

Collision Detection and Correction

Vagrant has built-in support for detecting port collisions, the case where a forwarded port definition would collide with another used port on your system.

By default, Vagrant will report an error so you can fix the issue by either freeing up that used port, or by changing the port in the Vagrantfile.

Alternatively, Vagrant can auto-correct the collision by choosing another port to use for you. This must be explicitly enabled because it is otherwise confusing when bringing up a new guest machine that the forwarded port defined may have changed, even though Vagrant tells you about the detected collisions and auto-corrections.

To enable auto-correction, add an extra option to your existing forwarded port definitions, like so:

```
config.vm.forwarded_port 80, 8080, auto_correct: true
```

If a port collision detection is detected for that forward port, Vagrant will then auto-correct it to some other unused port. By default, Vagrant will choose an auto-correction port between port 2200 and port 2250.

This range can also be customized with a setting in the Vagrantfile:

```
config.vm.usable_port_range = (2200..2250)
```

TCP versus UDP

Forwarded ports by default only work with TCP connections. If you need to forward UDP packets as well, you have to configure an additional forwarded port with UDP port forwarding:

```
config.vm.forwarded_port 80, 8080, protocol: "udp"
```

This forwarded port will only forward UDP packets. If you want to allow both protocols, two forwarded port declarations must be used.

Host-Only Networking

Host-only networking creates a network that is private to your host and the guest machines on that host. Because this is a new, custom network, it has its own IP address space, so guest machines with host-only networking get their own IP.

Vagrant supports host-only networks by specifying a static IP for the machine. Vagrant will handle creating the host-only network and configuring the guest machine to get the specified IP.

The machine can then be accessed directly using this IP. This is a benefit over forwarded ports, since you can then access all the ports directly on the guest machine, rather than enumerating each one on an as-needed basis.

Pros and Cons

"Host-only" literally means that only the host machine and the guest machines can access this network. Machines outside of the host, such as other machines on the local network, cannot access the assigned static IP. This is both a pro and a con.

The pro of the isolation of host-only networks is that they're secure. Outside computers have no way of accessing network services you may be running.

The con is that because it is isolated, coworkers and team members who may be working on the same project can't look at your work. The most common use cases for this are testing web pages on mobile, showing a coworker a bug or feature, and so on. This can't be done with host-only networks.

Another benefit of host-only networks is that multiple virtual machines can communicate with each other by being a part of the same network. With forwarded ports, a virtual machine can't talk to another virtual machine. With host-only networking, as long as the machines are on the same network and know each other's IP addresses, they can communicate! The primary use case for this is separating services onto multiple virtual machines to more accurately mimic production, such as web servers and database servers.

In addition to multiple virtual machines being able to communicate, the virtual machines can also communicate with the host itself. This can be useful for accessing services running on the host machine. Forwarded ports, on the other hand, can only be accessed from the host machine. The guest can't talk to the host.

Networking multiple virtual machines together will be covered in detail in Chapter 5.

Basic Usage

Configuring a host-only network is done in the Vagrantfile as usual with a single line:

```
config.vm.network "hostonly", "192.168.33.10"
```

This is the first time seeing this configuration directive. The `config.vm.network` directive configures networking on the machine. By passing `hostonly` in as the first argument, a host-only network will be created. The second argument is the static IP to assign to the machine.

This static IP can be anything, although according to RFC specifications, a private, reserved network range should be used.

After configuring the Vagrantfile, create the guest machine or run `vagrant reload` with a running guest for Vagrant to configure the new network.

When the machine comes back up, it will be accessible with the configured static IP. You can verify this with a `ping`:

```
$ ping 192.168.33.10
PING 192.168.33.10 (192.168.33.10): 56 data bytes
64 bytes from 192.168.33.10: icmp_seq=0 ttl=64 time=0.412 ms
64 bytes from 192.168.33.10: icmp_seq=1 ttl=64 time=0.259 ms
64 bytes from 192.168.33.10: icmp_seq=2 ttl=64 time=0.364 ms
64 bytes from 192.168.33.10: icmp_seq=3 ttl=64 time=0.275 ms
...
```

In addition to being able to access the guest, the guest itself is able to access the host machine. This is very useful it the host itself is running services that may be useful for the guest machine. The IP address of the host is always the same IP address but with the final octet as a 1. In the preceding example, the host machine would have the IP address 192.168.33.1. This can be verified by connecting with SSH into the guest machine and pinging:

```
$ vagrant ssh
vagrant@precise64:~$ ping 192.168.33.1
PING 192.168.33.1 (192.168.33.1) 56(84) bytes of data.
64 bytes from 192.168.33.1: icmp_req=1 ttl=64 time=0.197 ms
64 bytes from 192.168.33.1: icmp_req=2 ttl=64 time=0.216 ms
64 bytes from 192.168.33.1: icmp_req=3 ttl=64 time=0.378 ms
64 bytes from 192.168.33.1: icmp_req=4 ttl=64 time=0.346 ms
...
```

Guest Operating System Dependency

For each operating system, there are different methods of configuring network devices. Unfortunately, across multiple operating systems, these methods are inconsistent.

Vagrant has built-in knowledge of how to configure networks for a variety of operating systems such as Ubuntu, FreeBSD, Solaris, and more. When booting a machine, Vagrant probes the guest to determine the operating system, and uses this knowledge to do the right thing.

The downside of this is if you're running an operating system within Vagrant that Vagrant has no knowledge of, then host-only networking cannot be used. In these cases, a bug should be reported to the project.

Bridged Networking

Bridged networking bridges the virtual machine onto a device on your physical machine, making the virtual machine look like another separate physical machine on the network.

Vagrant supports bridged networking by enabling it and allowing the network to which the machine is bridged to use DHCP to assign an IP to the guest machine.

Because the machine appears to be a physical machine on your network, it is accessible by any machine on your network. Likewise, it adheres to any network routing rules and protections that may exist from routers, firewalls, and so on. As an example of this, home and work routers generally don't allow inbound connections through, so the bridged virtual machine cannot be accessed by the global Internet. However, these routers generally do allow access to machines on the local network, so your mobile device or a coworker's machine can access the virtual machine as long as they are all connected to the same network.

Pros and Cons

Bridged networking gives you all the benefits of having an IP to access your virtual machine, just like a host-only network. But unlike host-only networks, there is no isolation, so you can use your mobile device to view websites served from the guest machine, you can share your work with coworkers, and so on.

This lack of isolation can also be seen as a downside, if that is a necessary requirement for your project.

One downside of bridged networking with Vagrant is that Vagrant doesn't currently allow you to specify a static IP for the bridged network. IP addresses from bridged networks are served via DHCP, so you must SSH into the guest machine and inspect the network configurations in order to determine the IP to access the machine. Host-only networks, on the other hand, have predictable static IP addresses.

Another downside of bridged networking is that because the guest must adhere to the network rules in place by the router, bridged networking simply has no benefits for some environments. Most commonly, hotel and airport networks restrict communication between machines on the local network, so even with the IP of the guest machine, you are unable to communicate. In these situations, there is simply no benefit to using a bridged network, and a host-only network must be used.

Basic Usage

Bridged networking is enabled within the Vagrantfile with a single line:

```
config.vm.network "bridged"
```

This tells Vagrant to enable a bridged network device for the virtual machine. The IP is served from DHCP so there are no other configuration options here.

When running `vagrant up` or `vagrant reload` for the bridged network to take effect, Vagrant will ask you what network you want the device bridged to. If you don't know what to answer here, you probably want to choose the same device that is connected to the Internet.

In the following `vagrant up` output, my laptop was connected to the Internet via WiFi at the time, so I choose to bridge onto my wireless networking device, making my virtual machine appear on the WiFi network:

```
$ vagrant up
Bringing machine 'default' up with 'virtualbox' provider...
[default] Importing base box 'precise64'...
[default] Matching MAC address for NAT networking...
[default] Setting the name of the VM...
[default] Clearing any previously set forwarded ports...
[default] Creating shared folders metadata...
[default] Clearing any previously set network interfaces...
[default] Available bridged network interfaces:
1) en0: Wi-Fi (AirPort)
2) p2p0
3) vnic0
4) vnic1
What interface should the network bridge to? 1
[default] Preparing network interfaces based on configuration...
[default] Forwarding ports...
[default] -- 22 => 2222 (adapter 1)
[default] Booting VM...
[default] Waiting for VM to boot. This can take a few minutes.
[default] VM booted and ready for use!
[default] Configuring and enabling network interfaces...
[default] Mounting shared folders...
[default] -- /vagrant
```

Because the IP address is served from DHCP, we need to inspect the network configuration from within the virtual machine in order to determine the IP address it was given. For Ubuntu, the box we're currently using, we do this as follows:

```
$ vagrant ssh
vagrant@precise64:~$ ifconfig
eth0      Link encap:Ethernet  HWaddr 08:00:27:88:0c:a6
          inet addr:10.0.2.15  Bcast:10.0.2.255  Mask:255.255.255.0
          inet6 addr: fe80::a00:27ff:fe88:ca6/64 Scope:Link
          UP BROADCAST RUNNING MULTICAST  MTU:1500  Metric:1
          RX packets:332 errors:0 dropped:0 overruns:0 frame:0
          TX packets:225 errors:0 dropped:0 overruns:0 carrier:0
          collisions:0 txqueuelen:1000
          RX bytes:40678 (40.6 KB)  TX bytes:31408 (31.4 KB)

eth1      Link encap:Ethernet  HWaddr 08:00:27:60:3e:01
          inet addr:10.0.1.31  Bcast:10.0.1.255  Mask:255.255.255.0
          inet6 addr: fe80::a00:27ff:fe60:3e01/64 Scope:Link
```

```
              UP BROADCAST RUNNING MULTICAST  MTU:1500  Metric:1
              RX packets:10 errors:0 dropped:0 overruns:0 frame:0
              TX packets:9 errors:0 dropped:0 overruns:0 carrier:0
              collisions:0 txqueuelen:1000
              RX bytes:1216 (1.2 KB)  TX bytes:1494 (1.4 KB)

lo            Link encap:Local Loopback
              inet addr:127.0.0.1  Mask:255.0.0.0
              inet6 addr: ::1/128 Scope:Host
              UP LOOPBACK RUNNING  MTU:16436  Metric:1
              RX packets:0 errors:0 dropped:0 overruns:0 frame:0
              TX packets:0 errors:0 dropped:0 overruns:0 carrier:0
              collisions:0 txqueuelen:0
              RX bytes:0 (0.0 B)  TX bytes:0 (0.0 B)
```

A bit of experience helps here, but Vagrant generally sets up the second adapter as the bridged adapter. This is not always the case, however, so use your knowledge of the network to which you're bridging to recognize the proper IP address that may be assigned.

In the example output, eth1 is the bridged device, and 10.0.1.31 is the IP address. We can verify that this device is actually bridged onto our network by pinging it:

```
$ ping 10.0.1.31
PING 10.0.1.31 (10.0.1.31): 56 data bytes
64 bytes from 10.0.1.31: icmp_seq=0 ttl=64 time=0.696 ms
64 bytes from 10.0.1.31: icmp_seq=1 ttl=64 time=0.330 ms
64 bytes from 10.0.1.31: icmp_seq=2 ttl=64 time=0.521 ms
64 bytes from 10.0.1.31: icmp_seq=3 ttl=64 time=0.286 ms
64 bytes from 10.0.1.31: icmp_seq=4 ttl=64 time=0.329 ms
^C
--- 10.0.1.31 ping statistics ---
5 packets transmitted, 5 packets received, 0.0% packet loss
round-trip min/avg/max/stddev = 0.286/0.432/0.696/0.155 ms
```

As you can see, the ping was successful, indicating the host is reachable. And while it isn't shown with a simple ping, the host being pinged is in fact the virtual machine that is running.

 As mentioned in "Pros and Cons" on page 60, bridged networking often fails on public networks or under certain router configurations. If vagrant up gets stuck on configuring the networking interfaces, this is likely what is happening.

Composing Networking Options

Each of the networking options comes with its own set of pros and cons. Individually, they're all equally useful in various use cases. Together, they're useful for every use case.

Vagrant allows you to enable multiple network options. As long as the guest machine has room for additional network interfaces (the limit in VirtualBox is eight), then Vagrant will configure it.

To enable multiple networks, just define multiple networks in the Vagrantfile:

```
config.vm.forwarded_port 80, 8080
config.vm.network "hostonly", "192.168.33.10"
config.vm.network "bridged"
```

Upon reading a Vagrantfile with this configuration, Vagrant would create a forwarded port mapping, create a host-only network with a static IP, and create a bridged network.

In addition to specifying multiple types of networks, it is possible to define multiple networks of the same type, such as specifying multiple host-only networks with different IPs.

NAT Requirement As the First Network Interface

With VirtualBox, Vagrant requires the first network device attached to the virtual machine to be a NAT device. The NAT device is used for port forwarding, which is how Vagrant gets SSH access to the virtual machine.

Therefore, any host-only or bridged networks will be added as additional network devices and exposed to the virtual machine as "eth1," "eth2," and so on. "eth0" or "en0" is generally always the NAT device.

It isn't currently possible to override this requirement, but it is important to understand that it is in place.

What's Next?

Networking is a key feature for using Vagrant in the most effective way. In this chapter, we showed the multiple options Vagrant gives you to network the guest machine in order to work the way you want to work.

The three networking options exposed by Vagrant cover almost all the use cases needed for networking with the guest machine.

With networking automated with Vagrant, team members who run a vagrant up now not only get shared folders, automated provisioning, and an isolated environment, but also get a way to access the machine using their own tools, such as web browsers. For many employees, such as designers or managers, this means that they never have to SSH into the virtual machine.

This is a powerful concept that makes the entire development process run more smoothly.

In the next chapter, we're starting to head toward more advanced features of Vagrant with multimachine clusters. These clusters allow you to model multiple machines with a single Vagrantfile, and are very popular with splitting different services out to different machines to better represent production environments.

CHAPTER 5

Modeling Multimachine Clusters

Modern web applications are created using multiple distinct parts, sometimes known as services. At the most common level, this is seen with the separation of a web and database server. There can also be cache services, worker queues, and more. Complex websites are often created with hundreds of these services.

When websites are designed this way, it is often called a service-oriented architecture.

As explained in "The Tao of Vagrant" on page 4, Vagrant is supposed to provide the developer with a complete development environment when `vagrant up` is run. In some cases, this means multiple machines are required or preferable as part of a single development environment.

Historically, development on these sorts of applications was done by cramming all of the required services down onto one machine. This isn't ideal for many reasons. First, this isn't how the services exist in production, so it is easy to have things work in development in a way they don't work in production, quickly leading to "works on my machine" bugs. Second, it is very difficult to test failure scenarios in development. What happens if a node in a cluster dies? What happens if there is too much backlog in the worker queue?

Vagrant lets you accurately model these scenarios using a feature called multimachine environments, which builds multiple virtual machines based on one Vagrantfile.

This is useful for properly isolating separate services as they are in production. You can then put your web server and database server in two separate virtual machines. It is trivial, in this case, to simulate network failure and observing how your application responds.

Of course, running many virtual machines is taxing on the computer, and there is a reasonable limit to the number of virtual machines that can be run at any given time.

Because of this, some strategy must be taken to determine what services will be separated and onto how many virtual machines.

Running Multiple Virtual Machines

Before getting started, make sure you run `vagrant destroy` to destroy any preexisting virtual machines. This step is required because in the process of defining multiple virtual machines in the Vagrantfile, Vagrant can lose the preexisting running machine. This is a bug that will be addressed in future versions of Vagrant. For now, destroying all virtual machines prior to configuring multiple machines will avoid this issue.

Next, we have to configure the Vagrantfile to include a second machine. For an example, we'll model a web and database server throughout this chapter:

```
Vagrant::Config.run do |config|
  config.vm.box = "precise64"

  config.vm.define "web" do |web|
    web.vm.forward_port 80, 8080
    web.vm.provision :shell, path: "provision.sh"
  end

  config.vm.define "db" do |db|
    # We'll fill this in soon.
  end
end
```

A lot of this should look familiar, while a lot of it is also very new. The part configuring the box should be familiar. But the configuration directive `config.vm.define` is new. This is the directive that defines a new machine within a single Vagrantfile.

It takes one parameter, which is the name of the machine. It then takes a block that configures that specific machine. You may notice that this looks very similar to the normal Vagrantfile configuration. That is because it is actually the same!

The block when defining a new submachine is just another configuration block that you see when creating a Vagrantfile. The `web` and `db` variables are full configuration variables where you can override any value for that machine.

Prior to getting a chance to override configuration values, submachines inherit the generic configuration. In the case of the preceding example, both the web and db machines will be made with the precise64 box because `config.vm.box` was set to precise64 in the outer configuration.

If you are a developer, you can think of all of this interaction as variable scopes within programming languages. The outer configuration is a more global scope than the inner submachine configuration, so the submachine can override values from the outer scope.

Before we bring up the Vagrant environment, make sure to set up the *provision.sh* script from Chapter 3, or remove the provisioning line from the web machine. I just put it there as a convenience for setting up Apache as we did in prior examples, but it isn't necessary for the example.

When you're ready, run `vagrant up`:

```
$ vagrant up
Bringing machine 'web' up with 'virtualbox' provider...
[web] Importing base box 'precise64'...
[web] Matching MAC address for NAT networking...
[web] Setting the name of the VM...
[web] Clearing any previously set forwarded ports...
[web] Creating shared folders metadata...
[web] Clearing any previously set network interfaces...
[web] Preparing network interfaces based on configuration...
[web] Forwarding ports...
[web] -- 22 => 2222 (adapter 1)
[web] -- 80 => 8080 (adapter 1)
[web] Booting VM...
[web] Waiting for VM to boot. This can take a few minutes.
[web] VM booted and ready for use!
[web] Configuring and enabling network interfaces...
[web] Mounting shared folders...
[web] -- /vagrant
[web] Running provisioner: VagrantPlugins::Shell::Provisioner...
stdin: is not a tty
Installing Apache and setting it up...
Bringing machine 'db' up with 'virtualbox' provider...
[db] Importing base box 'precise64'...
[db] Matching MAC address for NAT networking...
[db] Setting the name of the VM...
[db] Clearing any previously set forwarded ports...
[db] Fixed port collision for 22 => 2222. Now on port 2200.
[db] Creating shared folders metadata...
[db] Clearing any previously set network interfaces...
[db] Preparing network interfaces based on configuration...
[db] Forwarding ports...
[db] -- 22 => 2200 (adapter 1)
[db] Booting VM...
[db] Waiting for VM to boot. This can take a few minutes.
[db] VM booted and ready for use!
[db] Configuring and enabling network interfaces...
[db] Mounting shared folders...
[db] -- /vagrant
```

Things should look familiar, but instead of bringing up one machine, Vagrant brought up two. This is evident from the machine name prefix Vagrant puts on the output. You can see both [web] and [db] in the output.

Controlling Multiple Machines

The moment multiple machines are introduced into a Vagrant environment, the behavior of vagrant commands change a little bit.

Most commands, such as up, destroy, and reload now take an argument with the name of the machine to affect. As an example, if you wanted to reload just the web machine, you could do this:

```
$ vagrant reload web
...
```

By specifying no arguments, Vagrant assumes you want to take action on every machine. So vagrant reload alone would reload both the web and db machines.

For some commands, this default behavior of taking action on every machine doesn't make sense. vagrant ssh can't SSH you into every machine in one terminal! So some commands require a target machine.

The output of vagrant status changes, too. It now lists multiple machines and the state of each of them:

```
$ vagrant status
Current machine states:

web                       running (virtualbox)
db                        running (virtualbox)

This environment represents multiple VMs. The VMs are all listed
above with their current state. For more information about a specific
VM, run `vagrant status NAME`.
```

For detailed information on the state of a machine as well as helpful instructions on how to change the state of the machine, just call vagrant status with a target machine:

```
$ vagrant status web
Current machine states:

web                       running (virtualbox)

The VM is running. To stop this VM, you can run `vagrant halt` to
shut it down forcefully, or you can run `vagrant suspend` to simply
suspend the virtual machine. In either case, to restart it again,
simply run `vagrant up`.
```

In cases where the environment has many machines, you can specify multiple targets in the same command:

```
$ vagrant reload node1 node2 node3
...
```

Or, if you're managing many nodes, you can even use a regular expression. Vagrant assumes if the node name starts and ends with / that it is a regular expression. For example:

```
$ vagrant reload /node\d/
...
```

Although the command interface changes slightly, the behavior of commands upon individual machines is unchanged. Everything continues working as you'd expect, only now Vagrant manages multiple machines!

Communication Between Machines

If multimachine environments were made to model service-oriented architectures, there needs to be a way for the machines to communicate with each other. By default, by simply defining the machines, there is no way for them to communicate.

Host-Only Networks

By defining a host-only network on the machines that exists on the same subnet, the machines are able to communicate with each other. When specifying a static IP address with host-only networks on Vagrant, Vagrant by default uses a subnet mask of 255.255.255.0. This means that as long as the first three parts (octets) of the IP address are the same, the machines will be placed on the same network.

Let's modify the Vagrantfile so the machines can communicate. The Vagrantfile should look like this now:

```
Vagrant::Config.run do |config|
  config.vm.box = "precise64"

  config.vm.define "web" do |web|
    web.vm.forward_port 80, 8080
    web.vm.provision :shell, path: "provision.sh"
    web.vm.network :hostonly, "192.168.33.10"
  end

  config.vm.define "db" do |db|
    db.vm.network :hostonly, "192.168.33.11"
  end
end
```

The two machines are configured with host-only configurations that give them static IP addresses on the same subnet. You can tell they're on the same subnet because the first three octets are the same (i.e., 192.168.33). Reload the machines with `vagrant reload` to bring in the new networking configuration.

After the machines come back, you should be able to talk to each of them via their IP addresses. You can verify this with `ping`:

```
$ ping 192.168.33.10
PING 192.168.33.10 (192.168.33.10): 56 data bytes
64 bytes from 192.168.33.10: icmp_seq=0 ttl=64 time=0.488 ms
64 bytes from 192.168.33.10: icmp_seq=1 ttl=64 time=0.425 ms
64 bytes from 192.168.33.10: icmp_seq=2 ttl=64 time=0.433 ms
64 bytes from 192.168.33.10: icmp_seq=3 ttl=64 time=0.431 ms
...

$ ping 192.168.33.11
PING 192.168.33.11 (192.168.33.11): 56 data bytes
64 bytes from 192.168.33.11: icmp_seq=0 ttl=64 time=0.565 ms
64 bytes from 192.168.33.11: icmp_seq=1 ttl=64 time=0.513 ms
64 bytes from 192.168.33.11: icmp_seq=2 ttl=64 time=0.529 ms
64 bytes from 192.168.33.11: icmp_seq=3 ttl=64 time=0.415 ms
```

Furthermore, if you SSH into one of the machines, you will be able to talk to the other. As an example, let's SSH into the web machine and talk to the db machine, again via `ping`:

```
$ vagrant ssh web
vagrant@precise64:~$ ping 192.168.33.11
PING 192.168.33.1 (192.168.33.1) 56(84) bytes of data.
64 bytes from 192.168.33.1: icmp_req=1 ttl=64 time=0.271 ms
64 bytes from 192.168.33.1: icmp_req=2 ttl=64 time=0.317 ms
64 bytes from 192.168.33.1: icmp_req=3 ttl=64 time=0.291 ms
64 bytes from 192.168.33.1: icmp_req=4 ttl=64 time=0.262 ms
...
```

Success!

Using host-only networks, the two machines are able to communicate, so if one machine were running a service (e.g., a database), the other could connect to it.

Bridged Networks

In addition to host-only networking, multiple machines can communicate with bridged networking as well, technically, as long as they are all bridged onto the same device. In this case, you'll have to manually look up the IP that the router gives to the machines and communicate that way. This is not ideal, however. The preferred method of communication between machines in a multimachine environment is host-only networking.

Real Example: MySQL

Now that the basics have been covered, we'll provision the second machine with the shell provisioner to install MySQL on the second machine, and talk to that MySQL instance from the web machine using the MySQL client.

First, create a new file *db_provision.sh* in your project root with the following contents:

```
export DEBIAN_FRONTEND=noninteractive
apt-get update
apt-get install -y mysql-server
sed -i -e 's/127.0.0.1/0.0.0.0/' /etc/mysql/my.cnf
restart mysql
mysql -uroot mysql <<< "GRANT ALL ON *.* TO 'root'@'%'; FLUSH PRIVILEGES;"
```

This is the shell script that will provision the db machine. Let's quickly explain a few parts because it looks considerably different than the script used to set up Apache.

First, we export an environmental variable DEBIAN_FRONTEND with the value "noninteractive." This makes it so that when installing MySQL server, it does not ask us questions for a root password and all that.

Next, we use sed to replace the bind address from loopback to 0.0.0.0, which means all interfaces. This is necessary so that remote machines can connect to the server.

Then, we restart MySQL so that our configuration changes can take effect.

And finally, we tell MySQL to allow root to connect from any host. This is generally very unsafe, but for the purpose of this example, it will work well.

Let's wire it all up in the Vagrantfile with networking, and also by provisioning the web machine with the MySQL client. The Vagrantfile should look like this:

```
Vagrant::Config.run do |config|
  config.vm.box = "precise64"

  config.vm.define "web" do |web|
    web.vm.forwarded_port 80, 8080
    web.vm.provision :shell, path: "provision.sh"
    web.vm.provision :shell, inline: "apt-get install mysql-client"
    web.vm.network :hostonly, "192.168.33.10"
  end

  config.vm.define "db" do |db|
    db.vm.provision :shell, path: "db_provision.sh"
    db.vm.network :hostonly, "192.168.33.11"
  end
end
```

At this point, you should be able to fully understand the contents of the Vagrantfile. If there are any parts that are confusing or unclear, reread the previous sections until you fully understand them.

Run vagrant destroy to fully destroy both machines if they were running before. We want to start from a clean slate for this example.

After destroying the environment, run vagrant up to bring up both machines. This should take a few minutes, as both machines must fully provision.

Once the machines are running, log in to the web machine via SSH and use the MySQL client to access the db machine. The output should look similar to the following, but may be slightly different depending on versions and so on:

```
$ vagrant ssh web
vagrant@precise64:~$ mysql -uroot -h192.168.33.10
Welcome to the MySQL monitor.  Commands end with ; or \g.
Your MySQL connection id is 48
Server version: 5.5.29-0ubuntu0.12.04.2 (Ubuntu)

Copyright (c) 2000, 2012, Oracle and/or its affiliates. All rights reserved.

Oracle is a registered trademark of Oracle Corporation and/or its
affiliates. Other names may be trademarks of their respective
owners.

Type 'help;' or '\h' for help. Type '\c' to clear the current input statement.

mysql>
```

Success! The web machine is able to connect to a remote MySQL server, except that the remote MySQL server is actually just another virtual machine on the local system.

Given this example, it should be clear to see how these concepts can apply to larger or more complex architectures.

What's Next?

Vagrant multimachine environments paired with host-only networks are a powerful feature that can be used to test complicated multimachine architectures.

Running multiple virtual machines on your computer can be very resource intensive, so in general no more than a couple are run at any given time. However, it is a great way to test various production edge cases (e.g., failed networks).

Next, we're going to take a closer look at boxes, the base images that Vagrant creates the virtual machines from. We'll cover what they are, how they're made, and why you might want to make your own.

CHAPTER 6

Boxes

Boxes are the base images upon which Vagrant environments are built. So far in the book, we've been using a prebuilt box that has 64-bit Ubuntu 12.04 LTS installed. However, a box can contain any operating system installation, and new boxes can easily be created.

There are many reasons to create custom boxes. Primarily, you'll want any box you use to match the same environment you're running in production. So if you're running the application you're developing on FreeBSD in production, you'll want FreeBSD in development as well.

Additionally, organizations with very complicated software dependencies that can sometimes take an hour or more to install will sometimes "prebake" their boxes with the software installed. For example, if your application relies on Java, instead of installing Java on every `vagrant up`, you could install Java into the base image and already have it available. This saves precious time for creating the Vagrant environment.

Boxes can be created automatically from existing Vagrant environments, or manually from existing non-Vagrant managed VirtualBox virtual machines. In this chapter, we'll cover both processes, as well as talk about what boxes are and how Vagrant manages them.

Why Boxes?

First, let's discuss the rationale behind boxes. It is a fair question to ask why Vagrant doesn't just install an operating system automatically.

Boxes are an optimization so that Vagrant doesn't have to install a complete operating system on every `vagrant up`. Installing an operating system from scratch generally takes up to 30 minutes on a good computer.

Instead, Vagrant uses snapshotted base images to start with a pre-created base, and then builds on top of it. Base images generally don't change often.

This method makes Vagrant environments disposable. A `vagrant destroy` and `vagrant up` cycle to get a new environment generally takes only a few minutes.

In addition to being a basic optimization, it is another step to enforce and ensure that everyone working with the same Vagrant box starts with an identical base image.

Finally, boxes are portable. A box packaged on Mac OS X should work properly on Windows as well as Linux.

Box Format

The box file format is nothing more than a tar file, possibly gzip compressed.

The custom *.box* extension is meant to signify that it is meant to be used with Vagrant more than anything else, and to allow some flexibility in the future if Vagrant decides to change underlying formats.

The contents of the box file for VirtualBox is just the output of exporting a VirtualBox virtual machine. If you uncompress the precise64 box file, you'll see contents similar to the following:

```
$ tree
.
├── Vagrantfile
├── box-disk1.vmdk
├── box.ovf
└── metadata.json

0 directories, 4 files
```

The VMDK and OVF file are results of exporting a VirtualBox machine. VirtualBox has a function to "export" machines, which simply compresses the virtual hard disks and creates a portable definition of the virtual hardware required to run the virtual machine. The VMDK file is the compressed hard drive, and the OVF file is a description of the virtual hardware running the machine.

The Vagrantfile is just a normal Vagrantfile. As discussed in "The Vagrantfile" on page 17, this file is loaded and merged in the process of loading your project Vagrantfile. Having a Vagrantfile in a box is optional, but allows box creators to set some defaults up for Vagrant that can be overridden by the user.

The *metadata.json* file is just a basic JSON file that tells Vagrant what system the box works with (in this case VirtualBox).

When importing a VirtualBox box, Vagrant looks for a *box.ovf* file and tells VirtualBox to import that. The OVF file itself points to the VMDK file (and possibly other files that were part of the export), so that VirtualBox knows how to re-create the entire virtual machine.

Basic Box Management with Vagrant

Vagrant manages boxes globally per user, rather than per project like a project Vagrant-file. So, unlike `vagrant up`, `vagrant ssh`, and most other Vagrant commands, the commands to manage boxes affect every Vagrant environment.

How Global is "Global"?

Vagrant puts all global state by default into the *~/.vagrant.d* folder, including boxes.

This means that when Vagrant manages boxes "globally," it actually means it manages boxes per user, by default.

Because boxes can be large (sometimes gigabytes), you can move this global state directory by setting the environmental variable `VAGRANT_HOME` to another directory.

Before diving into the exact commands that are run to manage boxes, let's first talk about the high-level box management concepts.

Boxes are mapped in Vagrant to a logical name. This name is up to you. This logical name is the mapping between the `config.vm.box` setting in a Vagrantfile and the actual box that is used to build the machine. Therefore, you can name a box whatever you'd like, but it must match the name in a Vagrantfile that you wish to start.

Without the logical name, the box files have no unique identifier. Boxes are just files. Therefore, it is important to descriptively name your boxes.

All box management is done via the `vagrant box` command. This command itself has various subcommands, as seen here:

```
$ vagrant box
Usage: vagrant box <command> [<args>]

Available subcommands:
     add
     list
     remove
     repackage

For help on any individual command run `vagrant box COMMAND -h`
```

These subcommands are likely fairly self-explanatory in their overall function, but we'll go over each one just to be sure.

The first box management command you'll likely encounter is to add a box. We've actually avoided doing this throughout the entire book by using `config.vm.box_url` within Vagrantfiles, which automatically adds a box for us for an environment if it is missing. But under the hood, it's doing the same thing as the following:

```
$ vagrant box add precise64 http://files.vagrantup.com/precise64.box
Downloading with Vagrant::Downloaders::HTTP...
Downloading box: http://files.vagrantup.com/precise64.box
Extracting box...
Cleaning up downloaded box...
Successfully added box 'precise64' with provider 'virtualbox'!
```

Once the box is added, it is available for use by the rest of your Vagrant environments. You only need to download a box once, then Vagrant reuses it for multiple environments. Since it is only a base image, it is cloned for each environment.

You can see all the boxes you have installed by listing them:

```
$ vagrant box list
precise64 (virtualbox)
```

Boxes at the minimum are a couple hundred megabytes, and when they're large can be many gigabytes. If you feel like you're not going to use a box anymore, you can remove it from your system in order to reclaim some disk space. This is done with `vagrant box remove`:

```
$ vagrant box remove precise64 virtualbox
Removing box 'precise64' with provider 'virtualbox'...
```

You can remove a box even if there are running Vagrant environments based on that box. The box is only used as an initial clone and is not needed after that. But note that if you destroy those running Vagrant environments, Vagrant will need the box again the next time you run `vagrant up`.

Finally, if you want to share a box with a coworker or friend and you lost the original box file, you can repackage a box using `vagrant box repackage`. This command produces no output, but will put a *package.box* file in your current directory. This file is identical to the original box file you downloaded.

Creating New Boxes from an Existing Environment

The easiest way to create new boxes is using an existing Vagrant environment as a starting point.

This method is used to create new boxes that have more preinstalled software than their previous base. Therefore, if you want to support a new operating system, or a new bare-bones image, you'll want to read the next section which instead creates new boxes from scratch.

Creating new boxes from an existing Vagrant environment is useful to preinstall and configure software in the base image so that `vagrant up` can be faster.

This is common practice for larger organizations where provisioning runs can take upward of an hour or more. This sort of provisioning time drastically reduces the disposability of Vagrant environments, harming a critical productivity boost of the tool.

To build a box from an existing environment, you'll first need an existing environment, so `vagrant up`! After doing this, install any software you'd like on the machine. For the purposes of this example, we're going to install *htop*, a nice command line utility for viewing the state of your system that isn't installed by default in the base Ubuntu images:

```
$ vagrant ssh
vagrant@precise64:~$ sudo apt-get install -y htop
Reading package lists... Done
Building dependency tree
Reading state information... Done
The following NEW packages will be installed:
  htop
0 upgraded, 1 newly installed, 0 to remove and 66 not upgraded.
Need to get 66.9 kB of archives.
After this operation, 183 kB of additional disk space will be used.
Get:1 http://us.archive.ubuntu.com/ubuntu/ precise/universe htop amd64 1.0.1-1
[66.9 kB]
Fetched 66.9 kB in 0s (119 kB/s)
Selecting previously unselected package htop.
(Reading database ... 51095 files and directories currently installed.)
Unpacking htop (from .../htop_1.0.1-1_amd64.deb) ...
Processing triggers for man-db ...
Setting up htop (1.0.1-1) ...
```

You can run `htop` if you want to see what it looks like and show that it is now installed in the running Vagrant environment.

Next, exit out of SSH and run `vagrant package`:

```
$ vagrant package
[default] Attempting graceful shutdown of VM...
[default] Clearing any previously set forwarded ports...
[default] Creating temporary directory for export...
[default] Exporting VM...
[default] Compressing package to: /private/tmp/v/package.box
```

The resulting `package.box` is now a new box based on the existing running Vagrant environment. If you add this box and run a new Vagrant environment based on it, `htop` will be installed!

"package" versus "repackage"

There is both a vagrant package and a vagrant box repackage command. To the Vagrant newcomer, the differences between these two may not be quickly apparent.

vagrant package takes the currently running Vagrant environment and packages it into a reusable box. The use case for vagrant package is to take a running Vagrant environment that was possibly modified from the original box by installing and configuring software, and packaging it into a reusable box for other people.

vagrant box repackage takes a box that was previously added and repackages it back into a box file that can be distributed. A running Vagrant environment has no effect on repackage, and repackaging can be done even without a running Vagrant environment. The use case for repackage is to get a box file back from a box you added using vagrant box add in the past.

Creating New Boxes from Scratch

Creating new boxes from an existing environment requires there to already be a box that you can build off of. If you want to create a box for a new operating system or configured in a way that no other box exists, then you'll have to create one from scratch.

This process is much more manual and much more time consuming, but generally doesn't have to be done often since once you have a base image, you can create new images from that using the technique covered in the previous section.

Creating the VirtualBox Machine

To create a box from scratch, create the virtual machine manually in VirtualBox itself, from the VirtualBox application.

You can configure this virtual machine in any way you'd like, but in general it is recommended that you use a dynamically resizing drive with a generous amount of disk space to start, something like 40 to 100 GB.

Additionally, if you plan on sharing this box, try not to set the default memory allocation too high. Users of Vagrant can always modify the RAM size later, so it is better to err on the side of caution, and use the minimum amount of RAM necessary for a pleasant experience. Usually, for bare-bones operating system installs, 360 to 512 MB is good.

Finally, disable audio, USB, and other nonessential peripheral controllers. Most applications don't need these auxiliary features and they just waste resources.

The only thing that Vagrant absolutely requires is that the first network device must be a NAT device. Vagrant uses this initial NAT device for setting up port forwards necessary for SSH. Without this properly configured, the VM will not boot.

With this all prepared, go ahead and start the virtual machine and install and configure the operating system you'd like.

Configuring the Operating System

Once the operating system is installed, you must configure some things if you want to work within Vagrant defaults.

First, a Vagrant user must exist. This is the default SSH user. You can always use another SSH user by specifying the config.ssh.username variable, so if you want to match production more closely, feel free to use any other user here, and set the configuration later.

Since Vagrant uses SSH, you must also make sure that an SSH server is installed and properly configured to run on system boot.

The SSH user must be configured to authenticate using public key authentication. Vagrant doesn't support SSH using a normal password. Again, if you want to work within Vagrant's defaults, you should set up the SSH user to authenticate using the insecure private key (*https://github.com/mitchellh/vagrant/tree/master/keys*) that ships with Vagrant. The insecure private key is "insecure" because it is public knowledge and is the default key used by Vagrant to authenticate SSH connections.

However, if you're creating a private box for yourself or your team, you may want to use a custom private key that is more secure. In this case, you can configure the con fig.ssh.private_key_path variable later to point to the proper private key.

If you decide to use the insecure private key, here is what it looks like to set up the user on a basic Linux system (note that you may need to change some paths if your SSH user is different or if the home directories are in a different path):

```
$ mkdir /home/vagrant/.ssh
$ chmod 700 /home/vagrant/.ssh
$ cd /home/vagrant/.ssh
$ wget --no-check-certificate 'https://raw.github.com/mitchellh/vagrant/master/
keys/vagrant.pub' -O authorized_keys
$ chmod 600 /home/vagrant/.ssh/authorized_keys
$ chown -R vagrant /home/vagrant/.ssh
```

Finally, the SSH user must also have privileges to sudo. More specifically, the SSH user must have permissions to use sudo without a password. Vagrant uses sudo quite a bit in configuring the virtual machine.

When configuring sudo, also make sure that requiretty is disabled. Vagrant runs commands without a TTY, so if sudo requires it, all commands will fail.

Installing VirtualBox Guest Additions

VirtualBox Guest Additions are additional kernel drivers and configuration so that the virtual machine can take advantage of VirtualBox features such as shared folders, improved networking performance, and more.

For many features of Vagrant to work, or more specifically many features of VirtualBox, these guest additions must be installed.

The exact process of installing the guest additions can vary from system to system. For Linux-based machines, you'll need to install the Linux kernel headers for your system as well as build tools. For Ubuntu, both of these can be retrieved using the standard package manager:

```
$ sudo apt-get install linux-headers-$(uname -r) build-essential
...
```

Next, insert the guest additions image by using the GUI and clicking the Install Guest Additions menu item, usually under the "Devices" menu. This will insert a virtual CD into the machine.

Mount this CD within your virtual machine and start the installation process. For Ubuntu, this looks like this:

```
$ sudo mount /dev/cdrom /media/cdrom
...
$ sudo sh /media/cdrom/VBoxLinuxAdditions.run
...
```

This process should be similar, but different, for other operating systems.

Additional Software

At this point, the bare minimum necessary for a box is complete. However, additional software can be installed to enable additional features within Vagrant.

If you want to support Chef or Puppet provisioning, you must install Chef or Puppet. Installation for each of these tools is out of the scope of this book, but there should be simple instructions within the documentation for each project.

If you want to support NFS shared folders, the NFS client must be installed. This can typically be found and installed using the package manager for your operating system.

Each of these is not required, but installing them will help make your box function with more Vagrant features.

Remove udev Rules

It is very common for Linux-based boxes to fail to boot initially. This is often a very confusing experience because it is unclear why it is happening. The most common case is because there are persistent network device udev rules in place that need to be reset for the new virtual machine.

To avoid this issue, remove all the persistent-net rules. On Ubuntu, these are the steps necessary to do this:

```
$ rm /etc/udev/rules.d/70-persistent-net.rules
$ mkdir /etc/udev/rules.d/70-persistent-net.rules
$ rm -rf /dev/.udev/
$ rm /lib/udev/rules.d/75-persistent-net-generator.rules
```

Minimizing the Final Box Size

Virtual machine images are big. On average, they're between 500 MB and 2 GB. Luckily, there are some easy optimizations that can be made prior to packaging the boxes to save a lot of disk space in the final package.

Start by removing any unnecessary packages from the system. These can always be reinstalled later by provisioners if the user of the box feels they're needed. Easy things to remove are build tools, linux-headers, man pages, and so on.

Next, fill the virtual hard drive with zeros and delete the zero-filled file. This fixes fragmentation issues with the underlying disk, which allows it to compress much more efficiently later. On Ubuntu, it looks like this:

```
$ dd if=/dev/zero of=/EMPTY bs=1M
...
$ rm -f /EMPTY
```

Make sure that creating the zero-filled file is the final thing you do prior to packaging, so that the hard drive is in a pristine state for packaging with optimal disk space efficiency.

Packaging It Up

The final step is to turn the VirtualBox virtual machine into a Vagrant box file.

Vagrant is able to do this for you by using vagrant package with the --base flag (the argument to the flag should be the name of the virtual machine in the VirtualBox GUI):

```
$ vagrant package --base my_new_box
[my_new_box] Clearing any previously set forwarded ports...
[my_new_box] Creating temporary directory for export...
[my_new_box] Exporting VM...
[my_new_box] Compressing package to: /private/tmp/v/package.box
```

package.box in the current directory is the resulting box. You can test it by adding it and bringing up a new environment with it. Everything should work.

Setting Vagrantfile Defaults

If you used any nondefaults when setting up your box, such as a custom SSH user or custom SSH key, you can set these defaults in a Vagrantfile that is packaged with the box.

This Vagrantfile will be loaded prior to the project Vagrantfile, and the settings will be merged, with the project Vagrantfile overriding any conflicting values. This allows boxes to set defaults, while still letting users override these defaults.

To do this, create a normal Vagrantfile anywhere on your system. For example, if you changed the SSH user to "custom_user", then you might create a Vagrantfile that looks like the following:

```
Vagrant::Config.run do |config|
  config.ssh.username = "custom_user"
end
```

Then, when packaging the box, tell Vagrant to use it as the packaged Vagrantfile:

```
$ vagrant package --base my_new_box --vagrantfile Vagrantfile
...
```

Of course, make sure "Vagrantfile" is a path to the Vagrantfile you created. In the case of the previous example, Vagrant would look for the Vagrantfile in the current directory.

Packaged Vagrantfiles and "vagrant init"

It is a common misconception to think that Vagrantfiles packaged with boxes become the Vagrantfiles that are created when vagrant init is called with that box.

This is not the case.

Instead, when Vagrant is configured to use the box, the Vagrantfile packaged with the box is loaded and merged with the settings set in the project Vagrantfile.

What's Next?

Boxes are one of the first places users of Vagrant need to customize when they start using Vagrant, since many people don't use Ubuntu as the operating system that runs their software.

Having a firm understanding of how boxes are managed, what the contents of a box is, and how to create new boxes is critical in mastering Vagrant.

This chapter introduced these important concepts and went into detail on multiple methods to create new boxes.

With this and all the content of the preceding chapters complete, you now know almost everything Vagrant has to offer out of the box. You certainly know enough to be effective with Vagrant.

In the next chapter, we're going to cover how plug-ins can be used to extend Vagrant in case you want to add some additional features to Vagrant itself.

CHAPTER 7

Extending Vagrant with Plug-Ins

Vagrant provides a strong core set of features. These features were built upon years of release cycles and feedback based on how people want to use Vagrant in the real world.

But Vagrant is a general-purpose tool, so in order to cover every use case imaginable, Vagrant exposes a powerful plug-in interface so that third-party developers can enhance the features of Vagrant.

There is no canonical list of available plug-ins at the moment. Plug-ins are generally found by simply searching on Google or some other search engine. So if you're looking for some specific functionality, try that first.

This chapter covers how plug-ins are managed and also how they're developed. Using plug-ins can be done by just about anyone, whereas developing plug-ins requires a strong understanding of the Ruby programming language.

 Plug-ins are developed by third parties and therefore make no guarantees about stability. Because they are running within Vagrant itself, it is very easy for a plug-in to crash Vagrant. If this happens, you can always uninstall the plug-in.

Extensible Features

Vagrant exposes many features that can be extended by plug-ins. The places where plug-ins can extend Vagrant is carefully controlled so that you know what plug-ins are capable of and so that future versions of Vagrant can make a better effort at maintaining backwards compatibility.

Plug-ins can add new commands to the vagrant program. For example, a plug-in might make vagrant ip tell you the static IP for a running Vagrant machine. Behavior like this is completely possible using a plug-in:

```
$ vagrant ip
10.30.30.10
```

Plug-ins can also add new configuration options for the Vagrantfile itself. This is typically used in conjunction with some other plug-in capabilities so that the plug-in can be fine-tuned by the user. For example, a plug-in can make this possible:

```
Vagrant::Config.run do |config|
  config.fire_missles.enable = true
end
```

Plug-ins can add new provisioners, in case you want to use something other than shell scripts, Chef, or Puppet. There are much more than those three configuration management tools out there, and Vagrant is able to integrate with all of them via plug-ins. Additionally, if your organization uses a custom, in-house software provisioning tool, you can enable Vagrant to use it. It ends up looking like this in your Vagrantfile:

```
Vagrant::Config.run do |config|
  config.vm.provision "my_custom_provisioner", option: "value"
end
```

Plug-ins are also able to add or change functionality within existing virtual machine manipulation events (e.g., `vagrant up`, `vagrant destroy`, etc.). As an example, it is possible for a plug-in to also configure DNS on your host machine during `vagrant up` so that you can visit a domain name to access your Vagrant machine.

Finally, plug-ins can add new guest-specific or host-specific functionality to Vagrant. As mentioned at earlier points in the book, some features of Vagrant rely on operating system specific behavior, such as mounting folders, configuring networks, enabling NFS, and so on. Vagrant comes with knowledge of many common operating systems, but is still missing many. Plug-ins are able to add new guest- and host-specific logic to Vagrant so that Vagrant can work with any operating system.

Managing Vagrant Plug-Ins

Plug-in management is a core feature of Vagrant, exposed as the `vagrant plugin` command. This command is responsible for installing, uninstalling, and listing plug-ins. Similar to `vagrant box`, this command has even more subcommands.

To install a plug-in, use the `vagrant plugin install` command with the name of the plug-in you want to install:

```
$ vagrant plugin install foo
Installing the 'foo' plugin. This can take a few minutes...
Installed the plugin 'foo (0.0.1)'!
```

Vagrant will install the plug-in and any dependencies it might have. It will also tell you the version it installed so you can verify it got the proper version with what the author of the plug-in might list.

In addition to installing by plug-in name, you can also install using a path to the actual plug-in file, if the author offers a download:

```
$ vagrant plugin install /path/to/foo.gem
Installing the 'foo' plugin. This can take a few minutes…
Installed the plugin 'foo (0.0.1)'!
```

You can further verify what plug-ins are installed by listing them:

```
$ vagrant plugin list
foo (0.0.1)
```

And if you need to uninstall the plug-in, you can use the uninstall command:

```
$ vagrant plugin uninstall foo
Uninstalling the 'foo' plugin…
```

That's all there is to it. Be sure to reference the README file or documentation of any plug-ins you may find on the Internet for any additional documentation for installing it.

Where Do the Plug-Ins Come From?

When installed by name, plug-ins are downloaded from the central, official RubyGems repository.

This detail is hidden from end users of Vagrant in order to keep things simple, but Vagrant plug-ins are packaged as RubyGems. This lets Ruby developers use the tools they are comfortable with and take advantage of the comprehensive Ruby ecosystem in order to develop high-quality Vagrant plug-ins.

The plug-in download from RubyGems is done over simple HTTP and should respect any standard http_proxy environmental variable settings.

Note, however, that RubyGems does allow arbitrary code to be executed when installing RubyGem packages. While this feature is rarely used, it can be a significant security risk to be aware of.

Plug-In Development Basics

Anyone can write a plug-in for Vagrant. Plug-ins are written in Ruby (*http://www.ruby-lang.org/*) and packaged using RubyGems (*http://rubygems.org/*). Familiarity with both is required. If you're comfortable with both Ruby and RubyGems, then you're ready to write a Vagrant plug-in!

Plug-In Definition

All plug-ins are required to have a definition. The definition contains important details about the plug-in, such as its name and the components it contains.

The definition is the first and only thing that Vagrant should find when loading your plug-in. It is the critical piece that makes Vagrant plug-ins future-proof to large Vagrant internal changes. The small plug-in definition looks like this:

```
class MyPlugin < Vagrant.plugin("2")
  name "My Plugin"
end
```

A definition is a Ruby class that inherits from `Vagrant.plugin("2")`. The 2 here is the major version of Vagrant that the plug-in is valid for. API stability is only promised for each major version of Vagrant, so this is an important part of the plug-in definition.

At a bare minimum, the definition must contain a name for the plug-in. If no name is present, then the rest of the plug-in will not be loaded.

The most important aspect of the plug-in definition is that it must *always* load, no matter what version of Vagrant is running. Theoretically, Vagrant version 87 (doesn't actually exist) would be able to load a version 2 plug-in definition. The `Vagrant.plugin` method for the superclass of the definition is the only call into Vagrant that should be made as part of the definition.

The remainder of the stability of the definition is achieved through clever lazy loading of individual components of the plug-in, and is covered shortly.

By being able to load the plug-in definition with any version of Vagrant, a future version of Vagrant will be able to kindly notify users that one or more of their plug-ins is out of date, rather than crashing spectacularly.

What Happened to Version "1" Plug-Ins?

The plug-in version in this book starts with version 2, but what happened to version 1? Actually, version 1 is a valid plug-in version, but is silently ignored and not loaded by Vagrant.

Vagrant version 1.1 (part of release cycle leading up to version 2) was the first version of Vagrant to support this new plug-in system. Prior to this, Vagrant didn't have a solid plug-in system in place that was future-proof against newer versions of Vagrant.

When Vagrant 1.1 was released, all Vagrant 1.0.x plug-ins instantly became incompatible with Vagrant and would crash the new release. To avoid this issue in the future, the new plug-in system was created. And for new plug-in developers, the API version starts at version 2.

Plug-In Components

Within the plug-in definition, a plug-in must advertise all components it adds to Vagrant. Vagrant uses this knowledge to load the components at the proper time if they're needed. It is also used to track what plug-ins provide what functionality, which can then be shown back to users of Vagrant.

An example of a plug-in defining some components is shown here:

```
class MyPlugin < Vagrant.plugin("2")
  name "My Plugin"

  command "run-my-plugin" do
    require_relative "command"
    Command
  end

  provisioner "my-provisioner" do
    require_relative "provisioner"
    Provisioner
  end
end
```

The example adds on to the plug-in definition made earlier in order to define a new Vagrant command and a new provisioner.

Before diving into the details of the how components are defined, verify that none of the Ruby syntax looks foreign to you. From a pure Ruby programming language standpoint, the definition should be completely understandable. If you're confused by any part of the syntax of the definition, you need to get more familiar with Ruby prior to writing a Vagrant plug-in.

Components are defined using a method call with the type of component being defined, such as `command` or `provisioner`. These method calls take some number of parameters, which varies from component to component. In general, the first parameter is always a name.

All components take a Ruby block argument (a type of callback) that must return the actual component implementation class. This block argument is where the clever lazy loading happens that ensures future-proofing plug-ins. The component block arguments should lazy load the actual file containing the implementation of the component, and then return this component. This is why there are `require_relative` calls within the component blocks.

This lazy loading is necessary because the actual dependencies and APIs that components implement and use are not stable across major Vagrant versions. A command implementation for Vagrant 2.0 likely won't work with Vagrant 3.0. But the *definition* is just plain Ruby that must always be forward compatible to future Vagrant versions. Therefore, each individual component must be lazy loaded.

The exact arguments each component definition requires and the way the implementation is done is specific to each component. In future sections, we'll cover each component in turn.

Error Handling

Error handling is one of the most praised features of Vagrant. Vagrant has always had a guiding principal with regards to stability that if the user sees a stack trace, it is a bug, whether the stack trace was a result of user error or not.

Plug-ins should strive to follow this principal as well, since the framework for graceful error handling is already in place within Vagrant.

By using built-in Vagrant error handling mechanisms, your error messages will end up looking like Figure 7-1.

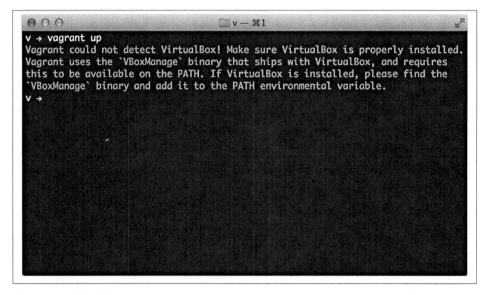

Figure 7-1. Nice Vagrant error messages

Error handling in Vagrant is done entirely by raising Ruby exceptions. Vagrant treats exceptions that inherit from Vagrant::Errors::VagrantError differently than others. If an exception inherits from VagrantError, then the vagrant command will output the message of the error in nice red text to the console and exit with an exit status of 1.

Otherwise, for any other exceptions, Vagrant reports an "unexpected error" with the complete stack trace. The Vagrant error messaging tells the user to consider these bugs, so you should do your best to use the built-in error handling mechanisms.

Here is an example of how to properly report errors. To start, define an exception class for that error somewhere:

```
class MyException < Vagrant::Errors::VagrantError
  error_message("Something bad happened!")
end
```

Then, raise the error at some point:

```
raise MyException
```

This will cause Vagrant to output "Something bad happened!" in red text when the exception is raised and exit with an exit status of 1.

Errors can also interpolate values in them. This is useful for putting data into the error message. Here's how the error is defined:

```
class MyException < Vagrant::Errors::VagrantError
  error_message("An error happened with '%{thing}'")
end
```

Then the additional values can be sent to the exception when it is raised. The value will be interpolated into the final error message:

```
raise MyException, thing: "a thing"
```

This would cause Vagrant to output "An error happened with *a thing*" and exit with an exit status of 1.

Vagrant Internals

An understanding of Vagrant internals will be necessary at some point while making a plug-in. It isn't necessary to study the entire source code or understand how Vagrant works on a deep level, but having a firm grasp of relevant Vagrant core classes is required for many plug-ins.

The Vagrant source code can be found on GitHub (*https://github.com/mitchellh/ vagrant*).

Relevant classes for certain components will be pointed out as we dive into detail for each component, but to get started, some useful classes to understand are Vagrant::En vironment and Vagrant::Machine.

A Basic Plug-In Development Environment

Before diving into how to build specific Vagrant components, let's set up a basic development environment for working on plug-ins.

While it would be great if we could use Vagrant to build the plug-in development environment, this isn't possible because VirtualBox can't run inside VirtualBox, and even if it could it would be far too slow. Instead, we'll set up a plug-in development environment on our own machine.

First, install Ruby and RubyGems. The exact process for this is out of the scope of this book. Windows users can use the RubyInstaller (*http://rubyinstaller.org/*). Mac OS X and Linux users will need to use their own respective package managers to get the proper version of Ruby. Vagrant plug-in development requires at least Ruby version 1.9.3. You can check the Ruby version by running `ruby --version`.

After this, install Bundler (*http://gembundler.com/*), which will be used to get the proper development version of Vagrant and to set up the dependencies for the plug-in itself (if it has any). You can verify Bundler is properly installed by running `bundle --version`, which should output the version of Bundler installed.

We'll use Bundler to set up the basic project directory, and unfortunately Bundler has a requirement on Git (*http://git-scm.com/*) for the gem specification. Git knowledge is *not* required to make Vagrant plug-ins, but install Git so that Bundler works properly. Again, this will differ by operating system, but a package or installer for Git is available for every major operating system and can be found from some basic searching.

At this point, we have all the tools installed on the machine to develop a Vagrant plug-in. Now let's set up the actual directory where work will be done.

As mentioned earlier, Vagrant plug-ins are packaged as RubyGems. Therefore, the same process for creating RubyGems applies to creating Vagrant plug-ins. Given this information, to set up our file structure, we can just use `bundle gem`, which sets up a basic development environment for a RubyGem:

```
$ bundle gem my_vagrant_plugin
      create  my_vagrant_plugin/Gemfile
      create  my_vagrant_plugin/Rakefile
      create  my_vagrant_plugin/LICENSE.txt
      create  my_vagrant_plugin/README.md
      create  my_vagrant_plugin/.gitignore
      create  my_vagrant_plugin/my_vagrant_plugin.gemspec
      create  my_vagrant_plugin/lib/my_vagrant_plugin.rb
      create  my_vagrant_plugin/lib/my_vagrant_plugin/version.rb
Initializating git repo in /private/tmp/example-plugin/my_vagrant_plugin
```

Now, go into the new directory created for your plug-in and modify the Gemfile to look like the following:

```
source "https://rubygems.org"

gemspec

group :development do
  gem "vagrant", :git => "git://github.com/mitchellh/vagrant.git"
end
```

This modifies the Gemfile to add a new "development" group that has Vagrant as a dependency sourced from the Git repository with the source.

Next, run `bundle` in order to get all the dependencies. After running `bundle`, you can verify things are working by running `bundle exec vagrant --version`. You'll see some warnings and maybe some errors about loading plug-ins from Vagrant. This is normal.

We'll next create a Vagrantfile that will be used to test our plug-in. The contents of the Vagrantfile should look like the following:

```
Vagrant.require_plugin "my_vagrant_plugin"

Vagrant::Config.run do |config|
  config.vm.box = "precise64"
end
```

The line containing `Vagrant.require_plugin` is most important. This tells Vagrant to explicitly load our development plug-in. This will let us test any new components we add to Vagrant.

Finally, create a basic plug-in definition in the root file for your plug-in. The root file is *lib/my_vagrant_plugin.rb* or more generically the Ruby file with the name of your RubyGem in the *lib/* folder.

This file is automatically loaded by Vagrant when the plug-in is installed, and should contain *only* the definition. Any other components should be lazy loaded in their definition section. For the example plug-in, the contents of *lib/my_vagrant_plugin.rb* look like the following:

```
module MyVagrantPlugin
  class Plugin < Vagrant.plugin("2")
    name "my vagrant plugin"
  end
end
```

This should all look very familiar based on what we've covered so far with regards to plug-in definitions. The only difference this time is that the plug-in definition is within a module. This isn't strictly required, but is generally good practice because then we namespace our components within this module as well and attempt to avoid any namespace conflicts later.

With all this set up, we're actually ready to start developing real components for the plug-in.

As a final check, run `bundle exec vagrant --version` to make sure Vagrant loads without any error. This will show that the plug-in is loading along with the definition. The output should look like the example below (it's possible that the version of Vagrant is different, depending on when you're reading this, which is OK:

```
$ bundle exec vagrant --version
You appear to be running Vagrant in a Bundler environment. Because
Vagrant should be run within installers (outside of Bundler), Vagrant
will assume that you're developing plugins and will change its behavior
in certain ways to better assist plugin development.

Vagrant version X.Y.Z
```

Should the Plug-In Depend on Vagrant?

The plug-in should *not* depend on Vagrant explicitly in the gemspec file. Vagrant plug-ins are meant to run only in the context of Vagrant, and possibly within any future version of Vagrant. For this reason, you can assume that the plug-in will run in Vagrant.

Even so, I typically add a check at the top of my plug-in definition file that looks something like this, just to verify we are actually running in Vagrant:

```
begin
  require "vagrant"
rescue LoadError
  raise "This plugin must run within Vagrant."
end
```

Developing a Custom Command

Plug-ins can add new commands to the vagrant program, exposing new functionality to Vagrant that did not exist before. These commands are able to manipulate the Vagrant virtual machine just like any other Vagrant command.

For our example plug-in, we'll add a free-memory command to Vagrant that will output the amount of free memory available in the virtual machine.

Component

The first thing to do is to augment the plug-in definition and add the command component to it. Modify the plug-in definition to look like the following:

```
module MyVagrantPlugin
  class Plugin < Vagrant.plugin("2")
    name "my vagrant plugin"

    command "free-memory" do
      require_relative "my_vagrant_plugin/command"
      Command
    end
  end
end
```

The command method is used to define a new command component for our plug-in. This is a simple method that takes a single parameter with the name of the command. In this example, the command will be available at vagrant free-memory when we finally implement it.

The block argument to the component loads the file containing the command implementation and returns the actual implementation class.

Implementation

The command implementation class inherits from Vagrant.plugin("2", "command"). This is a special method that returns the proper superclass for commands for version 2 of the plug-in API.

After inheriting from this class, the implementation for the commands is very straightforward. Commands only need to implement one method: execute. This method runs the command and returns the exit status for the command.

An initial implementation of the free-memory command is shown below. Note that at this point it doesn't do anything useful. We'll fix that in a moment. The implementation should go in the file *lib/my_vagrant_plugin/command.rb*:

```
module MyVagrantPlugin
  class Command < Vagrant.plugin("2", "command")
    def execute
      puts "Hello!"
      return 0
    end
  end
end
```

You can test the new command now by executing Vagrant within the bundler environment:

```
$ bundle exec vagrant free-memory
You appear to be running Vagrant in a Bundler environment. Because
Vagrant should be run within installers (outside of Bundler), Vagrant
will assume that you're developing plugins and will change its behavior
in certain ways to better assist plugin development.

Hello!
```

The typical plug-in development boilerplate shows up but so does the "Hello!" that is outputted from the execute method of the command! And if you check the exit status, it will be 0.

Congratulations! You just wrote your first visibly functioning Vagrant plug-in. In the next section, we'll make it a little bit more useful.

Working with the Virtual Machine

As a next step, we want to make the `fre-memory` command actually output the free memory amount within the virtual machine. To do this, we need to first verify the machine is actually running, and then we need to execute the command within the machine itself.

As a first pass, let's determine the state of the machine and output it to the user. We'll first show the code for the implementation, and then go over how it works following the example:

```
module MyVagrantPlugin
  class Command < Vagrant.plugin("2", "command")
    def execute
      machine = @env.machine(:default, :virtualbox)
      puts machine.state.id.to_s
      return 0
    end
  end
end
```

Within the `execute` method, we start by getting the machine object itself. This is done by asking the Vagrant environment for the default machine backed by VirtualBox.

`@env` is a helper available to all Vagrant commands that returns the current `Vagrant::Environment`. A `Vagrant::Environment` represents a single project directory and allows you to access the Vagrant configuration, machines for that project, state directories, and more.

`@env.machine` is a method that returns a `Vagrant::Machine` object for a given machine in the environment. It takes two parameters: the machine name and the machine provider. The name of the machine is "default" by default, and the only provider we've worked with in this book is VirtualBox. Both of these arguments must be Ruby symbols.

A `Vagrant::Machine` object represents a single Vagrant-managed guest machine for a Vagrant environment. It allows you to read the configuration, query the state, execute remote commands, manipulate the machine itself, and more.

In the command, we query the machine for its state and ask for the unique state ID. After that, the state ID is converted to a string and outputted to the user. The state ID is a single Ruby symbol distinctly identifying the state of the machine. Some examples of potential state IDs are `:not_created`, `:running`, and `:suspended`.

If we run this basic command in our environment, you should see something like the following:

```
$ bundle exec vagrant free-memory
You appear to be running Vagrant in a Bundler environment. Because
Vagrant should be run within installers (outside of Bundler), Vagrant
will assume that you're developing plugins and will change its behavior
in certain ways to better assist plugin development.

not_created
```

So it queried the state of the default machine and the state ID happens to be not_cre ated. Perfect! Now, we want to only query the free memory if the machine is running, so let's figure out what that state ID is. Run vagrant up to start running the machine, and when it is running, run vagrant free-memory again to determine the state:

```
$ bundle exec vagrant up
...
$ bundle exec vagrant free-memory
You appear to be running Vagrant in a Bundler environment. Because
Vagrant should be run within installers (outside of Bundler), Vagrant
will assume that you're developing plugins and will change its behavior
in certain ways to better assist plugin development.

running
```

Now that we know the state, we can add a guard to make sure that the machine is running before reading the free memory. This is just basic Ruby:

```ruby
module MyVagrantPlugin
  class Command < Vagrant.plugin("2", "command")
    def execute
      machine = @env.machine(:default, :virtualbox)
      if machine.state.id != :running
        @env.ui.error("Machine must be running.")
        return 1
      end

      return 0
    end
  end
end
```

One new thing in this example is using the env.ui object. This is an implementation of a Vagrant::UI::Interface. These UI objects properly handle output to the user, properly coloring it or hiding it depending on the environment that Vagrant is run in. A UI object should always be used instead of standard puts and gets that Ruby supplies. By calling env.ui.error, Vagrant will output the error message in the color red if the terminal supports colors.

Next, let's communicate with the machine in order to read the amount of free memory. The Vagrant::Machine object abstracts communication with the machine via a *communicator*, available using the Vagrant::Machine#communicate method.

Communicators provide a programmatically accessible shell. The transport mechanism is abstracted away, although it is usually SSH.

Using this communicator, it is quite easy to get the amount of free memory by calling the free command within the machine:

```
command = "grep MemFree /proc/meminfo | awk '{print $2}'"
machine.communicate.execute(command) do |type, data|
  @env.ui.info(data)
end
```

This reads the amount of free memory available and outputs it to the console. The command starting with "grep" is executing in the context of a shell on the guest machine. The data is then given in the callback. While we don't use the type variable, this variable is always either :stdout or :stderr depending on where the output is.

Putting this all together, our command implementation should now look like this:

```
module MyVagrantPlugin
  class Command < Vagrant.plugin("2", "command")
    def execute
      machine = @env.machine(:default, :virtualbox)
      if machine.state.id != :running
        @env.ui.error("Machine must be running.")
        return 1
      end

      command = "grep MemFree /proc/meminfo | awk '{print $2}'"
      machine.communicate.execute(command) do |type, data|
        @env.ui.info(data)
      end

      return 0
    end
  end
end
```

And if we run it, the output looks like what we want. The amount of free memory available in your virtual machine may be different. The number shown is the amount of free memory in kilobytes:

```
$ bundle exec vagrant free-memory
You appear to be running Vagrant in a Bundler environment. Because
Vagrant should be run within installers (outside of Bundler), Vagrant
will assume that you're developing plugins and will change its behavior
in certain ways to better assist plugin development.

278516
```

Working with Multimachine Environments

When working with the virtual machine in the previous section, we explicitly requested the "default" machine. In reality, this machine only exists if we're not in a multimachine environment.

In multimachine environments, the behavior of many of the Vagrant commands changes. Instead of working with the default machine, most commands in a multimachine environment work with every machine. If you have two machines defined, running vagrant up will bring up both. Additionally, you can pass the name of a specific machine to vagrant up, such as vagrant up web, and only that machine will be used.

Vagrant commands can get this behavior for free! Command implementation classes have access to a helper method called with_target_vms that reads an array of command-line arguments and figures out the right thing to do, giving the command the machines it needs to work with.

Let's enhance the free-memory command so that it uses this behavior. You may be surprised at how easy this becomes. Our command implementation becomes the following:

```
module MyVagrantPlugin
  class Command < Vagrant.plugin("2", "command")
    def execute
      command = "grep MemFree /proc/meminfo | awk '{print $2}'"

      with_target_vms(@argv) do |machine|
        if machine.state.id != :running
          env.ui.info("#{machine.name} is not running.")
          next
        end

        machine.communicate.execute(command) do |type, data|
          env.ui.info(data)
        end
      end

      return 0
    end
  end
end
```

Instead of explicitly calling env.machine to ask for a machine, the with_target_vms method is used, which yields machines to use. with_target_vms is given the arguments to the command, which are available at @argv in the command implementation class. This is an array of arguments. For example, if the command was called with vagrant free-memory foo bar baz, then @argv would be an array ["foo", "bar", "bas"].

Then, instead of exiting if a machine is not running, we just output to the user that the machine isn't running and move on. This way if there are multiple guest machines, we attempt to read the free memory for each of them.

Now, if you were to modify the Vagrantfile to have multiple machines, you could run vagrant free-memory and it would tell you the available memory in all of them or you could run vagrant free-memory TARGET and it would tell you the free memory in the target machine only.

Parsing Command-Line Options

So far, the command we've developed works great, but doesn't take any command-line flags. At some point, we may want to add the ability to add flags like --format or something similar.

Command-line option parsing is done using the optparse standard library that comes built into Ruby itself. This gives you the ultimate flexibility in controlling how command-line flags are interpreted. There is then a helper method available to all commands that takes an OptionParser instance and adds some sane defaults such as -h and --help processing.

Instead of adding flags to the free-memory command, let's just make sure there is useful help hooked up. By setting this up, it should become clear how to add additional flags.

Modify the execute method of the command implementation to look like the following:

```
opts = OptionParser.new do |o|
  o.banner = "Usage: vagrant free-memory [--help]"
end

argv = parse_options(opts)

command = "grep MemFree /proc/meminfo | awk '{print $2}'"

with_target_vms(argv) do |machine|
  if machine.state.id != :running
    env.ui.info("#{machine.name} is not running.")
    next
  end

  machine.communicate.execute(command) do |type, data|
    env.ui.info(data)
  end
end
```

All that is changed is the addition of the top section up to parse_options, and then replacing @argv with argv. As you can see, we just used a normal OptionParser. There is no magic happening here.

`parse_options` takes an `OptionParser` instance and parses the commands arguments according to those rules. It then returns the remaining positional arguments. This is why we pass `argv` back into `with_target_vms`.

Because this just works with a normal `OptionParser`, you can do anything you want with that instance to parse and set options for your command.

Adding New Configuration Options

Plug-ins can add new configuration sections that can be written in Vagrantfiles. This gives plug-ins the ability to have a Vagrant-standard way of configuring the plug-in from Vagrantfiles, and allows plug-ins to truly be first-class citizens within the Vagrant workflow.

Version "2" Configuration

Custom configuration keys are only available within version "2" Vagrant configurations. Throughout this book, we've used version "1" configuration because it has been stable for over a year and future versions of Vagrant are backward compatible with it.

Unfortunately, with Vagrant 1.1 and onward, there is no way to define plug-ins that extend version 1 configuration anymore. Therefore, any configuration plug-ins will be accessible in version 2 configuration only.

Version 2 configuration is very similar to version 1:

```
Vagrant.configure("2") do |config|
  # ...
end
```

Version 2 configuration and version 1 configuration can be intermixed within the same Vagrantfile, so you can continue using what you learned throughout this book while using V2 configuration where necessary.

Component

To define a new configuration key, the `config` method is used. Modify the plug-in definition to look like the following (if you've been following along from other sections, you should remove any prior components; we won't be building on top of existing examples to ensure that each plug-in development section is more useful as standalone reference material):

```
module MyVagrantPlugin
  class Plugin < Vagrant.plugin("2")
    name "my vagrant plugin"

    config "my_key" do
      require_relative "my_vagrant_plugin/config"
      Config
    end
  end
end
```

The `config` method is used to define a new configuration key component for the plug-in. It is a simple method that takes a single parameter with the name of the configuration key. In this example, the configuration plug-in will be exposed as `config.my_key` within Vagrantfiles.

The block argument to the component loads the file containing the configuration implementation and returns the actual implementation class.

After we're done with this section, we'll be able to have Vagrantfiles that look like this:

```
Vagrant.configure("2") do |config|
  # ... other stuff

  config.my_key.value = 12
end
```

Implementation

The configuration implementation class inherits from `Vagrant.plugin("2", "config")`. This is a special method that returns the proper superclass for commands for version 2 of the plug-in API.

After inheriting from this class, the implementation for configuration keys is very similar to a plain old Ruby object with attribute accessors.

For our configuration key, let's start by tracking a single option "value" which will be some numeric value. The initial implementation of this configuration key may look like the following:

```
module MyVagrantPlugin
  class Config < Vagrant.plugin("2", "config")
    attr_accessor :value
  end
end
```

It can't get much simpler than that! With just this, Vagrantfiles can now already contain references to `config.my_key.value`. You can verify this works by modifying the Vagrantfile in the plug-in working environment to set the value:

```
Vagrant.require_plugin "my_vagrant_plugin"

Vagrant.configure("2") do |config|
  config.vm.box = "precise64"
  config.my_key.value = 12
end
```

If you run a command like `vagrant up`, this will load this Vagrantfile without issue, proving that the configuration key is available, even if we're not doing anything with the value yet.

Accessing the Configuration

Now that we're able to set the configuration, we need a way to read it. The configuration is available in two places: on the `Vagrant::Environment` and on every `Vagrant::Machine`.

The difference between accessing configuration on the environment versus on the machine is simply a matter of scope. In single-machine environments, these two configurations actually end up being the same. In multimachine environments, each machine can override the configuration value. This can best be shown with an example:

```
Vagrant.configure("2") do |config|
  config.my_key.value = 1

  config.vm.define "A" do |a|
    a.my_key.value = 2
  end

  config.vm.define "B"
end
```

In this example, the value of "value" on the configuration object on the `Vagrant::Environment` would be 1. Within the configuration object on the `Vagrant::Machine` representing machine "A," the value would be 2. And on the configuration object on the `Vagrant::Machine` representing machine "B," the value would be 1 (since it inherited it from the global scope and didn't overwrite it).

In general, most plug-ins want to use machine-level scoping when reading configuration. The only time environment-level scoping is useful is if the configuration variable is meant to affect every machine in the environment, rather than each machine one-by-one.

On `Vagrant::Environment`, the configuration is available via the `global_config` attribute. For `Vagrant::Machine` objects, the configuration is available via the `config` attribute.

Configuration Merging

While the really basic configuration implementation made in the previous section appears to work, we actually need to change it a bit to make sure it plays nicely with the configuration merging system.

As you may know, whenever Vagrant is run, Vagrant reads multiple Vagrantfiles and configuration blocks and *merges* them all together to form the final configuration. This merging is most visible in multimachine environments, where each machine has a custom configuration scope that is merged with the parent scope.

In fact, Vagrant merges a handful of Vagrant configuration blocks every time it is run. Vagrant default configuration is just a hardcoded Vagrantfile that ships with Vagrant itself. This is the first Vagrantfile loaded. Then Vagrant loads Vagrantfiles for the user, the box being used, the project directory Vagrantfile, and then finally perhaps a submachine in a multimachine environment. For all of these cases, Vagrant must sanely merge configuration and do the right thing.

Luckily, this process is automated. As long as configuration implementations follow a few basic rules, it all automatically works, and Vagrant handles the complicated logic behind the scenes.

The only basic rule configuration implementations need to follow is to use UNSET_VAL UE as the default value for attributes, and then set the actual default value when the configuration is finalized. Let's show an example and then explain each piece. The following example modifies our previous configuration implementation to adhere to the basic merging rules:

```ruby
module MyVagrantPlugin
  class Config < Vagrant.plugin("2", "config")
    attr_accessor :value

    def initialize
      super

      @value = UNSET_VALUE
    end

    def finalize!
      @value = nil if @value == UNSET_VALUE
    end
  end
end
```

First, a constructor was added to the class in order initialize the "value" attribute. Prior to initializing the attributes, super is called to ensure that Vagrant can do any setup it may need to do.

The "value" attribute is then set to UNSET_VALUE, which is a special constant in Vagrant so that Vagrant can tell the difference between nil and an unset value. Because attributes are nil by default in Ruby, it is impossible for Vagrant to tell if the attribute was unset or if the user explicitly set the value to nil. This is important because if it was explicitly set to nil, we want the value to override a previous potentially non-nil value. UNSET_VALUE allows Vagrant to know whether the attribute was actually touched.

Next, the finalize! method is implemented. This method is called automatically by Vagrant to finalize the configuration. By calling this method, Vagrant is promising that all merging and configuration loading is complete, so the configuration can do whatever it needs to do to finalize itself.

In this case, we use the finalization method determine if the "value" attribute was never set, and if so, default it to nil. This is a very common pattern within Vagrant.

When merging two configurations, Vagrant goes through every instance variable in each configuration. If the configuration value in the newer configuration is anything other than UNSET_VALUE, then it overrides the previous configuration. Otherwise, the old value is retained.

Without these changes made, any newer configuration value of the "value" attribute would be nil, and would always overwrite the previous value, no matter what it was set to. Now, the configuration behaves correctly.

The automatic configuration merging logic Vagrant uses is generally what plug-ins wants almost every time.

There are, however, some cases where you want custom merging behavior. For example, in Vagrant core, synced folders are merged by appending the new synced folders to the old ones, rather than overwriting them.

If you need custom merging behavior, Vagrant lets you do that, too. As an example, let's change the merging behavior of "value" to inherit the newer value only if it is numerically larger than the old one. To do this, we override the merge method:

```ruby
module MyVagrantPlugin
  class Config < Vagrant.plugin("2", "config")
    # ... All the previous stuff we did.

    def merge(other)
      super.tap do |result|
        # Get the older and newer value
        older = @value
        newer = other.instance_variable_get(:@value)

        # Only if both values are set do we care about custom merging
        if newer != UNSET_VALUE && older != UNSET_VALUE
          if newer.to_i > older.to_i
            result.instance_variable_set(:@value, newer)
```

```
        else
          result.instance_variable_set(:@value, older)
        end
      end
    end
  end
end
```

There is a lot going on here, but at its core it is very simple. Take a moment to study the method. While it may be rare that a plug-in requires custom configuration merging, it is extremely important that the behavior is correct if custom merging is in place.

The `merge` method takes a single argument which is the other configuration object that is being merged. The result of the `merge` method should be a *new* configuration object (of the same class) properly merged. Therefore, `self` is the old configuration, `other` is the newer configuration being merged in, and the return value is the merged configuration. `other` is always an instance of the same class as `self`.

Within the `merge` method, it starts with a call to `super`. This invokes the default merging before of Vagrant. Then, by using `tap`, we modify the result of this default merging, returning the final modified value. This is another common pattern within configuration implementations in Vagrant.

The rest of the merge method is self-explanatory since it is just standard Ruby for our custom merge logic. We use `instance_variable_get` and `instance_variable_set` freely because it can be assumed that both configuration objects are the same structure.

And that concludes configuration merging. The default merging logic should be all you need most of the time, and by following simple rules and using `UNSET_VALUE`, the default logic works perfectly. However, if you need to tightly control the merging logic, Vagrant allows you to do that, too.

Private Variables and Configuration Merging

In some cases, configuration implementations track some state in instance variables that is ephemeral and not meant to be merged. If Vagrant sees that an instance variable starts with a double underscore (__), then it will ignore that instance variable.

This trick is commonly used with custom merge logic in order to avoid expensive object copies with the default merge logic prior to applying the custom logic (in the `super` call in the custom `merge` method).

For example, Vagrant core actually tracks synced folders in a `@__synced_folders` instance variable, since the merge logic is custom anyways, and it avoids copies of many large hashes.

Validation

Vagrant allows you to define validation rules for configuration implementations. If there are any validation errors, they are shown in a human-friendly way before Vagrant does anything. This avoids potential crashes later, which results in an overall better experience for the end user.

Configuration plug-ins can define their own custom validation rules to hook into this system by implementing the `validate` method.

The `validate` method is a plain old Ruby method that takes a `Vagrant::Machine` as a single parameter. This machine is the machine that the configuration will be applied to at some point. The availability of the actual machine object lets you access machine properties in order to determine different validation rules. The return value of `vali date` should be a Ruby hash where the keys are configuration sections, and the values are arrays of error message.

The `validate` method is called *after* the `finalize!` method, so you can assume all configuration values are finalized.

As always, an example explains best:

```
module MyVagrantPlugin
  class Config < Vagrant.plugin("2", "config")
    # ... All the previous stuff we did.

    def validate(machine)
      errors = []
                      if !@value
        errors << "Value must be set."
      end

      return { "my key" => errors }
    end
  end
end
```

In this example, we verify that `@value` is non-nil. Otherwise, we add an error to the list of errors, and we return the final mapping of sections to errors.

Adding a Custom Provisioner

Vagrant comes out of the box with support for some of the most popular provisioning systems available. But there are many dozens more publicly available, and many more custom solutions used privately by organizations. In order to accommodate all use cases, plug-ins can add support for new provisioners to Vagrant.

Provisioners are responsible for configuring the guest machine after boot. This typically involves automatically installing and configuring software in a repeatable, predictable way.

Component

To define a new provisioner component, the `provisioner` method is used. Modify the plug-in definition to look like the following (if you've been following along from other sections, remove any prior components; we won't be building on top of existing examples to ensure that each plug-in development section is more useful as standalone reference material):

```
module MyVagrantPlugin
  class Plugin < Vagrant.plugin("2")
    name "my vagrant plugin"

    provisioner "apt_get" do
      require_relative "my_vagrant_plugin/provisioner"
      Provisioner
    end
  end
end
```

The `provisioner` method is used to define new provisioners. It takes a single parameter with the name of the provisioner. This name is used when calling `config.vm.provision` in the Vagrantfile in order to enable the provisioner. With the previous example, the provisioner would be enabled by adding `config.vm.provision "apt_get"` to the Vagrantfile.

The block argument to the component lazily loads the file containing the provisioner implementation and returns the actual implementation class.

For the remainder of this section on custom provisioners, we'll be implementing a provisioner that uses `apt-get` to install a list of packages.

Implementation

The provisioner implementation class inherits from `Vagrant.plugin("2", "provisioner")`. This is a special method that returns the proper superclass for provisioners for version 2 of the plug-in API.

After inheriting from this class, the implementation only requires the provisioner to implement a single method: `provision`. The `provision` method is called automatically by Vagrant when the machine is created and able to be communicated with. It has no parameters and returns no values.

For our basic `apt-get` provisioner, the provisioner implementation may look like this:

```
module MyVagrantPlugin
  class Provisioner < Vagrant.plugin("2", "provisioner")
    def provision
      packages = ["htop", "curl"]
      command  = "apt-get install -y #{packages.join(" ")}"

      @machine.communicate.sudo(command) do |type, data|
        @machine.env.ui.info(data.chomp, prefix: false)
      end
    end
  end
end
```

The provisioner just has a static list of packages to install and runs `apt-get install` when it is time to provision. It also mirrors all the output back out to the UI so the user can see the status of the package install.

The `@machine` instance variable is available on all provisioners and is a reference to the `Vagrant::Machine` instance representing the machine being provisioned.

With just this in place, if you enable the provisioner in the Vagrantfile and run `vagrant up`, you should see it work. The Vagrantfile should look like this:

```
Vagrant.require_plugin "my_vagrant_plugin"

Vagrant::Config.run do |config|
  config.vm.box = "precise64"
  config.vm.provision "apt_get"
end
```

Then, running `vagrant up`, you should see the packages install:

```
$ bundle exec vagrant up
Bringing machine 'default' up with 'virtualbox' provider...
[default] Importing base box 'precise64'...
...
[default] Running provisioner: MyVagrantPlugin::Provisioner...
stdin: is not a tty
Reading package lists...

Building dependency tree...

Reading state information...

The following extra packages will be installed:
  libcurl3
The following NEW packages will be installed:
  curl htop libcurl3
0 upgraded, 3 newly installed, 0 to remove and 66 not upgraded.
Need to get 441 kB of archives.
After this operation, 1,094 kB of additional disk space will be used.
Get:1  http://us.archive.ubuntu.com/ubuntu/  precise/main  libcurl3  amd64
7.22.0-3ubuntu4 [237 kB]
```

```
Get:2    http://us.archive.ubuntu.com/ubuntu/    precise/main    curl    amd64
7.22.0-3ubuntu4 [138 kB]
Get:3 http://us.archive.ubuntu.com/ubuntu/ precise/universe htop amd64 1.0.1-1
[66.9 kB]
dpkg-preconfigure: unable to re-open stdin: No such file or directory
Fetched 441 kB in 0s (458 kB/s)
Selecting previously unselected package libcurl3.
(Reading database ...
51095 files and directories currently installed.)
Unpacking libcurl3 (from .../libcurl3_7.22.0-3ubuntu4_amd64.deb) ...
Selecting previously unselected package curl.
Unpacking curl (from .../curl_7.22.0-3ubuntu4_amd64.deb) ...
Selecting previously unselected package htop.
Unpacking htop (from .../htop_1.0.1-1_amd64.deb) ...
Processing triggers for man-db ...
Setting up libcurl3 (7.22.0-3ubuntu4) ...
Setting up curl (7.22.0-3ubuntu4) ...
Setting up htop (1.0.1-1) ...
Processing triggers for libc-bin ...
ldconfig deferred processing now taking place
```

Success! A fully functioning, albeit simple, provisioner.

Provisioner Configuration

While Vagrant has a strong belief in sane defaults so that things just work out of the box, Vagrant also allows almost every aspect of it to be tweaked via configuration options. This extends to provisioners, as well. Every built-in provisioner has additional configuration settings that can be set, and so can any provisioners from plug-ins.

Let's add some configuration for our apt-get provisioner so that the user can specify the list of packages to install.

Prior to reading this section, please become familiar with "Adding New Configuration Options" on page 101.

Provisioner configurations are just a special-case of normal configuration components within plug-ins. When defining the configuration component, make sure the name matches the provisioner name, and that there is a second parameter with the value of :provisioner. This tells Vagrant that this is a provisioner configuration component.

For our plug-in, the component looks like this:

```
module MyVagrantPlugin
  class Plugin < Vagrant.plugin("2")
    name "my vagrant plugin"

    config("apt_get", :provisioner) do
      require_relative "my_vagrant_plugin/provisioner_config"
      ProvisionerConfig
    end
```

```
      provisioner "apt_get" do
        require_relative "my_vagrant_plugin/provisioner"
        Provisioner
      end
    end
  end
```

Since the name of the configuration component matches the provisioner itself (apt_get), and the second parameter to the configuration component definition is :provisioner, Vagrant will connect the dots for us, and expose the provisioner when using config.vm.provision.

The implementation of the configuration itself is identical to the implementation of a typical configuration component. If this is unfamiliar, you can read more about it at "Implementation" on page 102. The configuration class is shown here:

```
module MyVagrantPlugin
  class Config < Vagrant.plugin("2", "config")
    attr_accessor :packages

    def initialize
      super

      @packages = UNSET_VALUE
    end

    def finalize!
      @packages = [] if @packages == UNSET_VALUE
    end
  end
end
```

With this in place, the provisioner can be configured in two ways. First, the shorthand method is available:

```
Vagrant::Config.run do |config|
  config.vm.box = "precise64"
  config.vm.provision "apt_get", packages: ["htop"]
end
```

Vagrant automatically translates any additional options sent to config.vm.provision into attribute setting on the configuration instance itself.

The longhand form is also available:

```
Vagrant::Config.run do |config|
  config.vm.box = "precise64"
  config.vm.provision "apt_get" do |p|
    p.packages = ["htop"]
  end
end
```

The benefit of the longhand form is if the configuration class exposes any methods, they can be called, whereas the shorthand form can only set attributes.

With the configuration definition and implementation in place, the next step is to actually access it. Provisioner configuration is exposed via the @config instance variable within the provisioner implementation. If a provisioner has no configuration defined, this will be nil, otherwise, it will be an instance of the configuration class for that provisioner.

The provisioner implementation can now be modified to install the packages specified by the user:

```
module MyVagrantPlugin
  class Provisioner < Vagrant.plugin("2", "provisioner")
    def provision
      command  = "apt-get install -y #{@config.packages.join(" ")}"

      @machine.communicate.sudo(command) do |type, data|
        @machine.env.ui.info(data.chomp, prefix: false)
      end
    end
  end
end
```

Instead of hardcoding the list of packages, @config.packages is used to get the list from the configuration.

Configuring the Machine

In addition to providing their own configuration, some provisioners need to configure the machine itself. For example, the Chef Solo provisioner needs to add synced folders to the machine so that the cookbooks become available within the guest machine.

Provisioners can implement a second method, configure, which is called early in the machine building process so that provisioners can configure the machine. The config ure method takes a single argument that is the root configuration for the machine. The provisioner can then add or modify to this configuration as necessary.

This sort of functionality isn't necessary for the apt-get provisioner we've built, but as an example, if you needed to sync the contents of a folder, you might add a synced folder:

```
module MyVagrantPlugin
  class Provisioner < Vagrant.plugin("2", "provisioner")
    # Other provisioner methods...

    def configure(root_config)
      root_config.vm.synced_folder "./files", "/files/on/guest"
    end
  end
end
```

This method is called early enough that *most* configuration values will take effect. Some values such as setting the box will have no effect.

Modifying Existing Vagrant Behavior

So far, every component discussed has only been able to *add* new behavior to Vagrant. You can add new commands, configuration keys, and provisioners. In addition to adding features, plug-ins can also modify existing Vagrant behaviors.

By modifying behavior, plug-ins can disable, modify, and add steps to a `vagrant up`, `vagrant destroy`, or almost any other Vagrant command. In many cases, this is done in conjunction with other plug-in components to provide a full feature set.

Component

Behavior modifications are done using a component called action hooks. Internally, Vagrant uses dozens of individual pieces called actions to build up more complicated functionality, such as a complete `vagrant up`. Therefore, the action hook component hooks into some portion of the action sequence to modify existing behavior.

Action hooks have a unique component definition. An example of one is shown here (if you've been following along from other sections, remove any prior components; we won't be building on top of existing examples):

```
module MyVagrantPlugin
  class Plugin < Vagrant.plugin("2")
    name "my vagrant plugin"

    action_hook("my_hook", "machine_action_up") do |hook|
      require_relative "my_vagrant_plugin/my_action"
      hook.prepend(MyAction)
    end
  end
end
```

The `action_hook` method is used to define new action hook components. It takes two parameters. The first parameter is the name of the action hook. This parameter isn't used currently except for debugging purposes, so just name it something descriptive. The second parameter is the name of the action sequence that you want to hook into. These will be covered in detail shortly.

Like other components, the `action_hook` method also takes a block that is responsible for lazily loading the actual implementations in use. But in this case, the block also takes an argument "hook" that is used to tell Vagrant where in the sequence of actions to hook into.

There is a lot happening here, so let's talk in more detail about each individual part.

First, the second parameter to the `action_hook` method: this is the name of the action sequence to hook into. Every major action sequence within Vagrant has a unique name. The most commonly used sequences are the `machine_action_` action sequences. in general, you can take almost any Vagrant command and prefix it with `machine_ac tion_` and that is the name of the action sequence you can hook into.

In the previous example, the plug-in is hooking into the `vagrant up` sequence of actions.

Unfortunately, the best way to find the full list of available action sequences is to read the source code of Vagrant itself (*https://github.com/mitchellh/vagrant*). Because Vagrant 2.0 is not out yet, the available action sequences can still actively change, so making an exhaustive list in this book isn't possible.

The next major part of the component is the "hook" object itself. This object has many methods on it to describe where to hook into the sequence of actions. In the example, we use the `hook.prepend` method. This tells Vagrant to prepend the action to the *beginning* of the action sequence. There is also `append` that looks and behaves similarly. All the methods on the "hook" object take an action implementation. These will be covered in the next section.

The "hook" object is actually an instance of `Vagrant::Action::Hook`. This is a very well-documented class. If you want to gain a deeper knowledge of the hook API, read the comments on it.

Implementation

Action implementations are simple, plain Ruby classes. Actions are modeled after Rack middleware (*http://stackoverflow.com/questions/2256569/what-is-rack-middleware*). They have an initializer that takes some arguments, and then implement the `call` method that is responsible for doing the actual work.

Actions don't need to inherit from any special Vagrant class.

In its simplest form, an action looks like this:

```ruby
module MyVagrantPlugin
  class MyAction
    def initialize(app, env)
      @app = app
    end

    def call(env)
      puts "--> Called!"
      @app.call(env)
      puts "<-- Called!"
    end
  end
end
```

The `initialize` method is given two arguments. The first is important—it is the next middleware to call. This should be stored in an instance variable for later. The second argument is the action environment, and is a hash of arbitrary state. This state is passed from action to action and is a way for actions to pass data to and from each other. This doesn't need to be stored and is only given to the constructor in case you want to set or use some initial state.

The actions are initialized all at once, prior to being called. No real logic should be done in the initialization method. Instead, this method should only be used for setting up basic state.

The `call` method is where the actual logic should go. This method is called by a previous action. The action should do what it needs to do in the `call` method. Most importantly, the action should also call the next action's `call` method. Recall that the next action was given as part of the `initialize` method. In the case of our example, this is done using `@app.call(env)`. It is also the responsibility to pass the action environment hash onward when calling the next action, as is done in the example implementation.

Because the next action can be called at any point in the `call` method, actions are able to do things both before and after the next action. The action to set up VirtualBox shared folders does this, for example, to set up the shared folder metadata before calling the next action, and then mounting the shared folders after calling the next action. This is because before calling the next action, the machine is still not booted, so metadata can be sent, and after calling the next action, the machine is booted, so the action can SSH in and mount folders.

Understanding the before and after semantics of actions is critical in order to use the full power of Vagrant action sequences.

At any point in the `call` method, the environment hash can be modified to add, modify, or remove state. Because this hash is passed through to the next action, the state is shared with every action, so be careful about choosing unique names for keys.

Let's view the implementation we have in action. Run `vagrant up` to see that the hook is properly called:

```
$ bundle exec vagrant up
Bringing machine 'default' up with 'virtualbox' provider...
--> Called!
[default] Importing base box 'precise64'...
[default] Matching MAC address for NAT networking...
[default] Setting the name of the VM...
[default] Clearing any previously set forwarded ports...
[default] Creating shared folders metadata...
[default] Clearing any previously set network interfaces...
[default] Preparing network interfaces based on configuration...
[default] Forwarding ports...
[default] -- 22 => 2222 (adapter 1)
```

```
[default] Booting VM...
[default] Waiting for VM to boot. This can take a few minutes.
[default] VM booted and ready for use!
[default] Configuring and enabling network interfaces...
[default] Mounting shared folders...
[default] -- /vagrant
<-- Called!
```

As you can see, at the top the action we defined outputs `--> Called!` then at the very end `<-- Called!` is output. This shows that the action is properly called, and also shows how the before and after semantics work with actions.

Useful Keys in the Action Environment

There are a set of useful keys that are always initially placed in the action environment so plug-ins can behave properly in the Vagrant environment. These are useful to know so that your actions don't struggle to figure out how to access certain information about the Vagrant environment, and don't attempt to query it in an incorrect way:

:box_collection

This is an instance of `Vagrant::BoxCollection` and represents the set of available boxes installed into the Vagrant environment. This can be used at any time to query, add, or remove boxes.

:global_config

This is the global configuration of the Vagrant environment. More information about what "global" means is described in "Accessing the Configuration" on page 103.

:host

This is an instance of the host implementation class. Although not covered too deeply anywhere in this book, Vagrant has many features that require doing operating system specific behavior on the host machine. To use these features, Vagrant detects the host operating system, and has built-in knowledge of how to do various things with that operating system. Not every operating system is supported, but most major operating systems are covered.

:gems_path

The path to which Vagrant plug-ins (packaged as RubyGems) are stored. This is useful when inspecting, installing, or removing gems.

:home_path

The path to the directory where Vagrant stores user-global state. This is, for example, where boxes are stored. This path can be used to store user-global state for your own plug-ins, if needed.

`:root_path`

> The path to the project root. This is commonly used for expanding relative paths because most relative paths in Vagrant are relative to the project root (where the project Vagrantfile is).

`:tmp_path`

> The path to the Vagrant temporary directory. This directory can be used to store temporary items, and Vagrant will ensure that they are properly removed (if it has operating system-level permissions to do so).

`:ui`

> The main UI object that should be used for input and output with the user.

When working with machine actions, such as `vagrant up`, some additional items are available in the action environment hash:

`:machine`

> The `Vagrant::Machine` object being modified. This can be used to query information about the machine such as the backing box, the configuration, SSH information, and so on.

`:machine_action`

> The action being invoked on the machine. This is usually something like `:up`, or `:destroy`. This can be used within your action to detect what is happening with the machine and change the behavior of the action where appropriate.

While these items are made available initially on the action environment, any action in the sequence can potentially modify or remove these items. No built-in Vagrant action will do this, and plug-ins are encouraged *not* to do this, but be aware that it can happen.

Learning More

Action sequences are the heart and soul of almost everything Vagrant does. Every interaction you have with Vagrant is done with action sequences. Furthermore, plug-ins can modify the behavior of almost everything Vagrant does because of this.

Due to their usage in almost every aspect of Vagrant internals, it is hard to list the actual sequences in use in this book because it is possible that they're still actively changing until version 2.0.

Therefore, the best place to learn more about action sequences is to read the source code of Vagrant itself (*https://github.com/mitchellh/vagrant*). If you plan on making any plug-in that modifies behavior using action hooks, this is highly recommended.

Other Plug-In Components

There are a few more things plug-ins are capable of that we didn't take the time to thoroughly explain in this chapter. Specifically, plug-ins are able to define new guest behavior, host behavior, and providers.

As mentioned at various points throughout the book, Vagrant is able to detect the host and guest operating system in order to do some operating system specific behavior. Vagrant has built-in knowledge of many of the major operating systems. But as a general-purpose tool, plug-ins are able to add new guest or host operating systems to Vagrant so that it can work on more platforms.

Adding new guest and host behavior is rare enough that it isn't worth discussing in great detail in this book. Additionally, the guest and host plug-in interface is about to undergo a major overhaul in its design, so any information about implementation specifics in this book would be quickly outdated. To avoid this, the topic is skipped entirely.

Providers are a particularly complex type of plug-in that allow Vagrant to control and manage machines that are backed by systems other than VirtualBox. Actually, Virtual-Box support itself is just a provider plug-in that ships with Vagrant. In addition to being complex, plug-in providers are relatively new to Vagrant, and may therefore still be changed quite a bit. To avoid immediately outdating this book, the topic is currently skipped.

Additional plug-in types are also planned prior to the official 2.0 release, so by the time you read this, other plug-ins may be possible.

The best place to learn about these additional plug-in components and how they're used is to read the Vagrant source code itself. Much of Vagrant is implemented through plug-ins itself, so you can see the official plug-ins that ship with Vagrant (*https://github.com/ mitchellh/vagrant/tree/master/plugins*).

Packaging the Plug-In

Up until this point, we've been locally developing the plug-in and testing it by using `bundle exec` to run Vagrant. When it's time to get this in the hands of actual users, however, we have to package it up so that they can use `vagrant plugin install` to install it. This section will cover the ins and outs of that process.

Plug-ins are packaged as RubyGems. The plug-in development environment we've been using has been set up so that it is simple to package and upload RubyGems. With just a few simple changes, the plug-in will be packaged in minutes.

First, we need to add "rake" as a development dependency to our environment. Rake is a Ruby framework for writing command line build tasks, similar to Make. We have to add it as a development dependency to the gem specification so that the Bundler environment will install it and make it available to us. To do so, add the following line to the *gemspec* file for the plug-in in *my_vagrant_plugin.gemspec*:

```
gem.add_development_dependency "rake"
```

In addition to adding "rake" as a development dependency, take a few moments to modify the description and summary fields of the gem specification. RubyGems won't allow us to build a gem that has "TODO" or "FIXME" in the descriptions.

After this, the entire gem specification should look something like this:

```
# -*- encoding: utf-8 -*-
lib = File.expand_path('../lib', __FILE__)
$LOAD_PATH.unshift(lib) unless $LOAD_PATH.include?(lib)
require 'my_vagrant_plugin/version'

Gem::Specification.new do |gem|
  gem.name          = "my_vagrant_plugin"
  gem.version       = MyVagrantPlugin::VERSION
  gem.authors       = ["Mitchell Hashimoto"]
  gem.email         = ["mitchell.hashimoto@gmail.com"]
  gem.description   = %q{Example Vagrant gem}
  gem.summary       = %q{Example Vagrant gem}
  gem.homepage      = ""

  gem.add_development_dependency "rake"

  gem.files         = `git ls-files`.split($/)
  gem.executables   = gem.files.grep(%r{^bin/}).map{ |f| File.basename(f) }
  gem.test_files    = gem.files.grep(%r{^(test|spec|features)/})
  gem.require_paths = ["lib"]
end
```

Next, run `bundle` so that "rake" is installed and added to the plug-in bundler environment. If you run `rake -T`, you should see that Bundler already exposes a set of tasks to create and release the gem:

```
$ bundle exec rake -T
rake build    # Build my_vagrant_plugin-0.0.1.gem into the pkg directory
rake install  # Build and install my_vagrant_plugin-0.0.1.gem into system gems
rake release  # Create tag v0.0.1 and build and push
  my_vagrant_plugin-0.0.1.gem to Rubygems
```

By running `rake build`, a packaged gem will be built:

```
$ bundle exec rake build
my_vagrant_plugin 0.0.1 built to pkg/my_vagrant_plugin-0.0.1.gem
```

You can verify that your plug-in works by going to a separate directory (to make sure we're outside of the bundler environment), and installing the plug-in into Vagrant using `vagrant plugin install`:

```
$ vagrant plugin install /path/to/pkg/my_vagrant_plugin-0.0.1.gem
Installing the '/path/to/pkg/my_vagrant_plugin-0.0.1.gem' plugin. This can take
a few minutes...
Installed the plugin 'my_vagrant_plugin (0.0.1)'!
```

Once you verify everything is working, `rake release` can be used to upload the RubyGem to the official RubyGems repository (*http://rubygems.org*). Note that you'll need to sign up for an account on the RubyGems.org website and that you *should not* release this example plug-in. Only release real plug-ins once they're ready.

Vagrant Environmental Variables

There are a handful of envrionmental variables you can set to control various aspects of Vagrant on your system. These environmental variables all have their uses, which are explained along with their function.

VAGRANT_CWD

VAGRANT_CWD can be set to change the working directory of Vagrant. By default, Vagrant uses the current directory you're in. The working directory is important because it is where Vagrant looks for the Vagrantfile. It also defines how relative paths in the Vagrantfile are expanded, since they're expanded relative to where the Vagrantfile is found.

This environmental variable is most commonly set when running Vagrant from a scripting environment.

As a simple example, if you wrote a bash script to bring up multiple Vagrant environments, it might look like this:

```
#!/usr/bin/env bash

VAGRANT_CWD=/foo vagrant up
VAGRANT_CWD=/bar vagrant up
```

VAGRANT_HOME

VAGRANT_HOME can be set to change the directory where Vagrant stores global state. By default this is set to ~/.vagrant.d, which is the .vagrant.d folder in your home folder.

The Vagrant home directory is where things such as boxes are stored, so it can actually become quite large on disk.

There are two common use cases for this environmental variable.

First, some people have small solid state drives as their main filesystem for speed, but also have a much larger, slower drive attached for larger files where speed doesn't matter as much. In this case, to save disk space on the expensive solid state drive, it makes sense to change VAGRANT_HOME to point to the much larger drive.

Another common use case is to isolate Vagrant installations for testing or scripting. The Vagrant home directory combined with the project *.vagrant* directory is all the state Vagrant uses to function. By specifying a new VAGRANT_HOME, Vagrant appears to be a clean installation.

VAGRANT_LOG

VAGRANT_LOG specifies the verbosity of log messages from Vagrant. By default, Vagrant does not store any logs.

Log messages are very useful when troubleshooting issues, reporting bugs, or getting support. At the most verbose level, Vagrant outputs basically everything it is doing.

Available log levels are "debug," "info," "warn," and "error." Both "warn" and "error" are practically useless since there are very few cases of these, and Vagrant generally reports them within the normal output.

"info" is a good level to start with if you're having problems, because while it is much louder than the normal output, it is still very human-readable and can help identify certain issues.

"debug" output is extremely verbose and can be difficult to read without some knowledge of Vagrant internals. It is the best output to attach to a support request or bug report, however.

VAGRANT_NO_PLUGINS

If VAGRANT_NO_PLUGINS is set to any value, then Vagrant will not load any plug-ins.

Plug-ins can introduce instability into Vagrant because it is just arbitrary third-party code. If you install a Vagrant that crashes Vagrant repeatably, then you can disable all plug-ins with this environmental variable.

VAGRANT_VAGRANTFILE

VAGRANT_VAGRANTFILE specifies the filename of the Vagrantfile that Vagrant searches for. By default, this is "Vagrantfile." Note that this is *not* a file path, but is just a filename.

This environmental variable is most commonly used in scripting environments where a single folder may contain multiple Vagrantfiles representing different configurations.

This variable is also used if you're testing new Vagrant configurations and don't want to mess up the old one. For example, if you were working in "Vagrantfile.new" temporarily until it is ready, you could test it like this:

```
$ VAGRANT_VAGRANTFILE=Vagrantfile.new vagrant up
...
```

Note that even while using a custom Vagrantfile name, Vagrant will still use the *.vagrant* directory in the project directory to store some local state. Therefore, it is not safe to run multiple Vagrant environments out of the same folder, and this environmental variable was not made for that purpose.

Vagrant Configuration Reference

This section serves as a complete reference to all the available configuration settings for Vagrant. As mentioned in "V1 versus V2 Configuration" on page 19, this section will only serve as a reference for V1 configurations, since V2 is not yet at a stable, unchanging state.

All settings are alphabetized so that they can be referenced more easily:

`config.nfs.map_gid`

Controls the global default GID mapping that is used for NFS shared folders. This should be set to an actual group ID (as a string) on the host system, or `:auto`. If the setting is `:auto`, Vagrant will automatically determine the group ID of the owner of any NFS shared folders and use that value. The default value is `:auto`.

`config.nfs.map_uid`

Controls the global default UID mapping that is used for NFS shared folders. This should be set to an actual user ID (as a string) on the host system, or `:auto`. If the setting is `:auto`, Vagrant will automatically determine the user ID of the owner of any NFS shared folders and use that value. The default value is `:auto`.

`config.package.name`

Controls the default filename of the output from `vagrant package`. This defaults to `package.box`.

`config.ssh.forward_agent`

Controls whether or not SSH connections enable agent forwarding. The default value is `false`.

`config.ssh.forward_x11`

Controls whether or not SSH connections will enable X11 forwarding. By default this is `false`.

`config.ssh.guest_port`

This is the port of the SSH daemon on the guest machine. This value is used when attempting to auto-detect the actual SSH port, when `config.ssh.port` is `nil`. One of the ways that Vagrant auto-detects the SSH port is by scanning the forwarded ports to see if any go to this guest port. If a forwarded port is found, Vagrant knows it can use that port for SSH. By default, this value is 22.

`config.ssh.host`

The host that Vagrant will connect to when attempting to SSH to communicate with the guest machine. This will override any detected value from Vagrant. This defaults to `nil`, allowing Vagrant to determine the host.

`config.ssh.max_tries`

The maximum number of tries that Vagrant will attempt to connect to the guest via SSH. Once this threshold is reached, Vagrant will show an error saying that SSh on the guest machine never became ready. By default, this is 30.

`config.ssh.port`

The port that Vagrant will use when connecting to the guest machine. If this is `nil`, Vagrant will attempt to auto-detect the correct port to use. Otherwise, this port will always be used, despite any detected SSH port by Vagrant. By default, this setting is `nil`.

`config.ssh.private_key_path`

The path to the private key file that Vagrant will use for SSH authentication. Vagrant only supports key-based authentication for SSH. If this value is a relative path, then it will be expanded relative to the project root directory. By default, this is set to the path to the insecure private key that ships with Vagrant.

`config.ssh.shell`

The shell that Vagrant will use to invoke any commands over SSH. Vagrant invokes all commands over SSH in the context of some shell. By default, this is `bash -l`. Be sure to specify any flags for login shells or anything that may be necessary when executing a command.

`config.ssh.timeout`

The timeout in seconds that Vagrant will use when attempting to make any SSH connection. Despite hitting this timeout, Vagrant attempts to retry connections `config.ssh.max_tries` number of times. This setting just lets attempted connections fail faster if it appears that SSH will never connect. The default value for this setting is 10.

`config.vagrant.dotfile_name`

The path where Vagrant will store local state about the project it is managing. Vagrant uses this state to track the IDs of the various guest machines that it is managing as well as any project-local state that may be necessary. If this path is relative, it will be expanded relative to the project root directory. By default, this is *.vagrant*.

`config.vagrant.host`

This provides a way to tell Vagrant what type of operating system the host machine is running. If this is `:detect` then Vagrant will automatically detect the host operating system and use the proper implementation. Otherwise, this can be set to a value such as `:arch` or `:windows`. This setting should only be used if Vagrant is unsuccessfully detecting the proper host. Even in this case, a bug should be reported to Vagrant.

`config.vm.auto_port_range`

This is a Ruby Range instance that defines the range of ports that Vagrant will use when it needs a free port to auto-correct a forwarded port collision. The default value is `2200..2250`.

`config.vm.base_mac`

The MAC address of the NAT device on a VirtualBox virtual machine. When using Vagrant with VirtualBox, this value is used to set the MAC address of the NAT device so that Internet connectivity properly works. This value should be set in all Vagrant box files for VirtualBox, so users don't need to worry about setting this on a per-project basis. If this isn't set, VirtualBox machines will not boot.

`config.vm.boot_mode`

This specifies the mode that the VirtualBox machine is booted into. There are two valid values: `:headless` or `:gui`. If the value is set to `:headless`, then no GUI will be shown when the virtual machine runs. The virtual machine process exists in the background. When the value is set to `:gui`, a full GUI is shown so you can inspect the boot process. The default value is `:headless`.

`config.vm.box`

The name of the box Vagrant will use when building the guest machine. This should map to the logical name of a box that exists from the `vagrant box list` command.

`config.vm.box_url`

The URL to where the box specified by `config.vm.box` can be found in case it isn't already installed on the system. This setting is optional and is only used if the box doesn't already exist on the user's system.

`config.vm.customize`

This allows you to use `VBoxManage` to customize the VirtualBox virtual machines Vagrant creates prior to them being booted. `VBoxManage` is a low-level command line interface that ships with VirtualBox and lets you control almost every aspect of the virtual machine, such as the amount of RAM, number of CPUs, virtual disk information, and more. Documentation on how to use this tool is outside the scope of this book, but there is official documentation online from the VirtualBox website (*http://www.virtualbox.org/manual/ch08.html*).

This setting is a method call. It can be called multiple times and Vagrant will apply the changes in the order specified. The parameter to the method is an array of arguments to send to `VBoxManage`. The special value `:id` is replaced with the UUID of the virtual machine for commands that require that as a parameter.

As an example, the following Vagrant configuration will set the amount of memory in the virtual machine to 1 GB:

```
Vagrant::Config.run do |config|
  config.vm.customize ["modifyvm", :id, "--memory", "1024"]
end
```

`config.vm.define`

This is a method used to define machines a multimachine environment. If you're unfamiliar with multimachine environments, refer to Chapter 5. The method takes two parameters: the name of the submachine and an optional second parameter with a hash of options. In addition to these parameters, a block can optionally be given to the call to define configuration specific to that submachine. The only available option to pass a second parameter is `:primary`. When set to `true`, that submachine is marked as primary, and calls to commands such as `vagrant up` without a target will use the primary.

`config.vm.forward_port`

This is a method used to define new forwarded ports on the guest machine. For more information on forwarded ports, see "Forwarded Ports" on page 55. This method can be called multiple times to define multiple forwarded ports. This method has two required parameters: the port on the guest and the port on the host that will forward to that port on the guest. The method also takes an optional third parameter which is a hash of additional options. The available options are:

- `:adapter`—This is the adapter number within VirtualBox that Vagrant will attach the forwarded port to. This defaults to the first adapter.

- `:auto`—If this is set to `true`, then Vagrant will automatically try to change the host port if it would collide with some other application using that port. If this is set to `false`, then Vagrant will show an error when it detects a collision. This defaults to `false`.

- :id—This is a unique identifier for the forwarded port. If this is set, then the settings of this forwarded port will override any previously set forwarded port with the same ID. Additionally, configuration read after this can override this forwarded port if the ID matches. The default SSH port that Vagrant forwards has an ID of ssh, allowing it to be overridden if necessary.

- :protocol—This specifies the protocol that the forwarded port will listen for. Allowed values are :tcp and :udp. This defaults to :tcp.

config.vm.guest

This specifies the operating system running in the guest machine. Vagrant uses this information to do operating system behaviors such as mounting folders and configuring networks. The value of this setting should be a symbol specifying the name of the guest implementation to use. This defaults to :linux. Another valid value is :freebsd.

config.vm.host_name

This can be set and Vagrant will set the hostname of the guest machine to this value. If this is nil, then no hostname will be set. This defaults to nil.

config.vm.network

This can be used to define network configurations for the guest machine. For more information on networking and the options Vagrant has for it, see Chapter 4. This method takes at least one parameter, which is the type of network to define. Available networking types are :hostonly and bridged. Depending on the type, additional parameters may be required or are available. The last parameter is always an optional hash of options. We'll go over the available options and parameters for each type of network next.

If the network type is :hostonly, then there is one additional parameter required. This parameter is the IP address to assign to the guest machine. Any IP address can be used here, but be careful because if an IP address you need to visit is actually used, then you'll no longer be able to access it because all traffic will go to the virtual machine. To be safe, you should only use IP addresses from any of the private IPv4 address spaces (*http://bit.ly/14cSLX1*). Instead of specifying an IP address, you can also specify :dhcp. This will cause the machine to use a custom DHCP server to get an IP address.

In addition to the required parameter, host-only networks can take an optional third parameter with a hash of options. The available options for host-only networks are:

- :adapter—This is the adapter number where the host-only network device will be attached to the VirtualBox machine. This defaults to nil, in which case Vagrant will automatically detect the next available device slot.

- :auto_config—This determines whether Vagrant will attempt to automatically configure the network device within the guest machine. By default this is true. If set to false, the network device will be attached to the guest machine, but will have to be manually configured within the guest.

- :mac—This specifies the MAC address of the network device. If this is nil, then Vagrant will generate a random MAC address. Otherwise, this should be set in the format of "aa:bb:cc:dd:ee:ff".

- :netmask—This specifies the subnet mask for the host-only network. All machines with IP addresses on the same subnet will be able to communicate with each other. By default, this is 255.255.255.0.

If the network type is :bridged, no additional parameters are required. However, an optional second parameter can be given which is a hash of additional options. The available options for bridged networks are:

- :adapter—This is the adapter number where the host-only network device will be attached to the VirtualBox machine. This defaults to nil, in which case Vagrant will automatically detect the next available device slot.

- :bridge—The full name of the network device to bridge to. If this isn't specified, or is nil, then Vagrant will ask the user what network they wish to bridge to when running vagrant up.

- :mac—This specifies the MAC address of the network device. If this is nil, then Vagrant will generate a random MAC address. Otherwise, this should be set in the format of "aa:bb:cc:dd:ee:ff".

config.vm.provision

This is used to enable and configure provisioners. For more information on provisioning, see Chapter 3. This method can be called multiple times to enable multiple provisioners. The provisioners will be run in the order enabled. Provisioners have one required parameter, which is the name of the provisioner to use. Valid values for this that are built into Vagrant are :shell, :chef_solo, :chef_client, :puppet, and :puppet_server. Additional provisioners may be available from plug-ins. After specifying the name, an optional second parameter can configure the provisioner. In addition to the optional second parameter, an optional block can be given for more advanced configuration of the provisioner. For more information, see the provisioner-specific documentation.

config.vm.share_folder

This is a method that defines or modifies shared folders on the guest machine. For more information on shared folders, see "Shared Filesystem" on page 25. This method can be called multiple times to share multiple folders. Shared folders have three required parameters. The first parameter is a unique ID for the shared folder definition. This has no meaning other than within configuration, so choose something short and descriptive. The second parameter is path to the folder on the guest machine that will have the shared folder. The third parameter is the path to the folder on the host machine that will be shared. The path on the guest machine must be an absolute path. The path on the host machine can be relative or absolute. If it is relative, it will be expanded relative to the project root directory.

There is also an optional fourth parameter that can be a hash of additional options. The available options for shared folders are:

- `:create`—If set to `true`, the folder on the host will be created if it doesn't exist. The default value is `false`.

- `:nfs`—If set to `true`, then the folder will be shared using NFS rather than the default VirtualBox shared folder mechanism. This can improve performance drastically in some cases. The default value is `false`.

- `:transient`—If set to `true`, then the shared folder definition will not be persisted across restarts. The default value is `false`.

When using NFS shared folders, a few additional options are recognized:

- `:map_gid`—The group ID that modifications to files on the guest will map to on the host. By default, Vagrant will use the GID of the owner of the folder.

- `:map_uid`—The UID that modifications to files on the guest will map to on the host. By default, Vagrant will use the UID of the owner of the folder.

- `:nfs_version`—The NFS version that will be used for the protocol for the mount. This defaults to 4.

Troubleshooting and Debugging

While thousands of companies and many more thousands of individuals worldwide use Vagrant everyday and praise Vagrant for being stable, there are issues that come up here and there. Vagrant is a complex software package built up of many moving pieces, so while we strive for perfection, this is hopefully understandable.

Luckily, there are multiple resources available for getting help.

When using any of the available Vagrant support resources, have a debug log ready showing the problem you may be running into. The debug log can be enabled by setting the VAGRANT_LOG environmental variable to debug. This will cause the output from Vagrant to be *extremely* loud. Copy this output and paste it into any code sharing website, such as a Gist (*http://gist.github.com*).

If you feel confident in attempting to solve the problem yourself prior to asking for help, you can also tweak the debug log to be slightly less loud to try to identify errors. The info level is usually best to get started.

On Linux systems, the environmental variable can be set by prepending Vagrant commands with it:

```
$ VAGRANT_LOG=debug vagrant up
...
```

On Windows systems, you must use set to set the environmental variable prior to running Vagrant commands:

```
> set VAGRANT_LOG=debug
> vagrant up
...
```

IRC

Internet Relay Chat (IRC) is a protocol for live chat messaging with a group of people. Vagrant has an active IRC channel with hundreds of users. You can often get a response to your issues by chatting in the IRC channel.

The Vagrant IRC channel is `#vagrant` on Freenode. Freenode is an IRC network available at `chat.freenode.net`.

The quality and availability of assistance through IRC largely depends on the time of day and who is currently active in the channel. Support is not guaranteed, but the channel is generally very helpful.

Mailing List/Google Group

For a less real-time solution, there is also a Vagrant mailing list via Google Groups. This allows you to post topics similar to a forum, and receive responses from any subscribed members.

The Vagrant mailing list has thousands of people who engage in active discussions daily. Since the support channel is very asynchronous, a response can take a day or sometimes many days. However, your inquiries will be seen by many more individuals over the mailing list than IRC.

The Google Group for Vagrant is named "vagrant-up" (*http://groups.google.com/group/vagrant-up*).

Professional Support

If you're integrating Vagrant into your workplace and want professional support, that is available as well. Professional support gives you access to guaranteed response times from individuals who work with Vagrant every day.

To learn more about the professional support packages, see the professional support page on the Vagrant website (*http://www.vagrantup.com/support/professional.html*).

Index

We'd like to hear your suggestions for improving our indexes. Send email to index@oreilly.com.

containers, 5

D

debugging (see troubleshooting)
defaults
    memory allocation, 78
    Vagrantfile, 82
destroy, 31
development environment, plug-ins, 91

E

environmental variables, 121–123
    Linux, 133
    VAGRANT_CWD, 121
    VAGRANT_HOME, 121
    VAGRANT_LOG, 122
    VAGRANT_NO_PLUGINS, 122
    VAGRANT_VAGRANTFILE, 122
error handling, plug-ins, 90
export, VirtualBox, 74

F

facter, 52
filesystem, shared, 25
format, boxes, 74
forwarded ports, 27, 55
free memory, 95

G

getting started example, 15–33
global state, 75
Google Groups, 134
guest additions, installing in VirtualBox, 80
guest operating system dependency, 59

H

halt, 30
help, 14
Hiera, 51
host-only networks, 57, 69

I

inline scripts, 48
installation
    Apache, 39

Vagrant, 8–13
VirtualBox, 7
VirtualBox guest additions, 80
IRC (Internet Relay Chat), 134

K

keys, 116

L

Linux
    environmental variable, 133
    installing Vagrant, 12
    VirtualBox installation, 7

M

Mac OS X, installing Vagrant, 9
mailing list, 134
memory allocation, 78
multimachine clusters, 65–72
    communication, 69
    controlling, 68
    MySQL, 70
    running, 66
multiple provisioners, 47
MySQL, 70

N

networking, 55–64 (see environmental variables)
    about, 26
    bridged networking
        about, 59–62
        communication between machines, 70
    composing network options, 62
    forwarded ports, 55
    host-only networks, 57, 69
    NAT requirement as the first network interface, 63
no provision mode, 48

O

OpenSSH, 24

P

package versus repackage, 78

About the Author

Mitchell Hashimoto is a passionate engineer, professional speaker, and entrepreneur. Mitchell has been creating and contributing to open source software for almost a decade. He has spoken at dozens of conferences about his work, such as VelocityConf, OSCON, FOSDEM, and more. Mitchell is the founder of HashiCorp, a company whose goal is to make the best DevOps tools in the world, including Vagrant. Prior to HashiCorp, Mitchell spent five years as a web developer and another four as an operations engineer.

Colophon

The animal on the cover of *Vagrant: Up and Running* is a blue rock pigeon (*Columba livia*).

The cover image is from Wood's *Animate Creations*. The cover font is Adobe ITC Garamond. The text font is Adobe Minion Pro; the heading font is Adobe Myriad Condensed; and the code font is Dalton Maag's Ubuntu Mono.

Have it your way.

Get even more for your money.

Join the O'Reilly Community, and register the O'Reilly books you own. It's free, and you'll get:

- $4.99 ebook upgrade offer
- 40% upgrade offer on O'Reilly print books
- Membership discounts on books and events
- Free lifetime updates to ebooks and videos
- Multiple ebook formats, DRM FREE
- Participation in the O'Reilly community
- Newsletters
- Account management
- 100% Satisfaction Guarantee

Signing up is easy:

1. Go to: oreilly.com/go/register
2. Create an O'Reilly login.
3. Provide your address.
4. Register your books.

Note: English-language books only

To order books online:

oreilly.com/store

For questions about products or an order:

orders@oreilly.com

To sign up to get topic-specific email announcements and/or news about upcoming books, conferences, special offers, and new technologies:

elists@oreilly.com

For technical questions about book content:

booktech@oreilly.com

To submit new book proposals to our editors:

proposals@oreilly.com

O'Reilly books are available in multiple DRM-free ebook formats. For more information:

oreilly.com/ebooks

O'REILLY®

Spreading the knowledge of innovators   oreilly.com

CPSIA information can be obtained at www.ICGtesting.com
Printed in the USA
BVOW05s1331180713

326331BV00001B/2/P